AF683350

Public Service Case File Packet

Cooper v. Cooper

Montane v. Hadden

PUBLIC SERVICE CASE FILE PACKET

Cooper v. Cooper
Montane v. Hadden

Mark S. Caldwell
Public Program Development & Resource Director
National Institute for Trial Advocacy

NITA
NATIONAL INSTITUTE FOR TRIAL ADVOCACY

© 2013 by the National Institute for Trial Advocacy

All rights reserved. No part of this work may be reproduced or transmitted in any form or by any means, electronic or mechanical, including photocopying and recording, or by any information storage or retrieval system without the prior written approval of the National Institute for Trial Advocacy unless such copying is expressly permitted by federal copyright law.

Law students who purchase this NITA publication as part of their class materials and attendees of NITA-sponsored CLE programs are granted a limited license to reproduce, enlarge, and electronically or physically display, in their classrooms or other educational settings, any exhibits or text contained in the printed publication or on the accompanying CD/DVD disk. However, sharing one legally purchased copy of the publication among several members of a class team is prohibited under this license. Each individual is required to purchase his or her own copy of this publication. *See* 17 U.S.C. § 106.

Address inquiries to:

Reprint Permission
National Institute for Trial Advocacy
1685 38th Street, Suite 200
Boulder, CO 80301-2735
Phone: (800) 225-6482
Fax: (720) 890-7069
E-mail: permissions@nita.org

ISBN 978-1-60156-323-1
FBA 1323

14 13 12 11 10 9 8 7 6 5 4 3 2 1
Printed in the United States of America

Contents

Cooper v. Cooper

Perceptions matter.

The subject matter of this case file includes a number of difficult issues, including domestic violence and alcohol. Both are serious problems in our culture. Recent statistics tells us approximately 1.3 million women and 835 thousand men were abused in the United States in the year preceding the writing of this problem. Over 18 million Americans were dependent upon alcohol. Chances are high that a member of the jury, or even the judge, may have personal experience with one or both of these problems.

Other perceptions matter as well. Jacob Cooper is approximately six feet tall and weighs 190 pounds. Some may consider Mr. Cooper a big man. However, the average weight of a man in the United States is currently 196 pounds.

Mr. Cooper has tattoos and was described as one of the "bad boys" when he was in high school. One in five Americans currently has a tattoo. Thirty-six percent of Americans in the age range of eighteen to twenty-five years have a tattoo. Forty percent of Americans who are between twenty-six and forty years old have tattoos. Having a tattoo may no longer be thought of as having a relationship with bad behavior.

In his book *Rewired: Understanding the iGeneration And the Way They Learn*, Larry Rosen suggests that the majority of those people classified as the iGeneration believe that multitasking, as done by Marcus Horton, is the most efficient use of their time. People categorized in this group are often bored when only performing a single task and believe they are effective at performing multiple tasks at once.

As you plan your case story, factual themes, and witness examinations, take care to appreciate what perceptions might be with your fact finder - be it judge or jury.

Introduction

This problem was written for use at NITA and other public service programs with the intent of helping lawyers and law students improve their trial skills. The focus of the problem is specifically on witness examination skills and storytelling as it relates to presenting factual information to judges and juries.

This matter is set for hearing to determine if a temporary restraining order should be extended into a permanent restraining order.

Jacob and Sara Cooper were married June, YR-2. The relationship has been stormy. In July, YR-1, Sara called the police and reported that Jacob had abused her. The police investigated but could not develop sufficient proof to charge Jacob as there were no signs of physical abuse. The police gave Jacob a warning and told him he did not want them to return. Since that time Jacob was arrested for driving under the influence and he pleaded guilty to driving while impaired. Sara has received a citation for shoplifting and accepted a deferred prosecution in the past two years.

Jacob is twenty-two years old. Sara has just turned twenty. They have no children. Jacob is employed as an assembly line worker at the Nita Cannery. Sara is not employed. Based upon Jacob's income they live below the poverty level. The Coopers receive public assistance in the form of food stamps and live in subsidized housing.

On the 6th day of Month-4, police were called to the Yankee Doodle Restaurant at 5th and Main Streets in downtown Nita City on a complaint of domestic violence. Police arrested both the Coopers when they were unable to determine who initiated the assault. The complaining witness, Marcus Horton, was one of the clerks behind the counter. He called the police immediately after the event occurred. In his statement to the police Mr. Horton indicated he heard a loud vocal disturbance from the dining area of the restaurant. When he looked over to the source of the noise he saw Mr. Cooper stand up and slap his wife across the face. Another witness from the restaurant, Debra Scott, told police she was sitting at the table next to the Coopers and overhead Mrs. Cooper cursing her husband and then watched her throw a bowl of oatmeal at Mr. Cooper and make other threatening gestures. In response, Mr. Cooper stood up and struck his wife.

Nita law requires police to make an arrest in the event of a domestic violence complaint. Because they could not determine who was at fault, and both the Coopers were legally intoxicated, they arrested both parties. The city attorney declined to prosecute either party under the criminal statutes of Nita.

On the 7th day of Month-4, the Coopers were released after spending the night in the "drunk tank." No charges were pressed for their public intoxication. Mrs. Cooper went immediately to the Nita Battered Woman's Shelter and sought counseling. She applied for a temporary restraining order the next day and the court granted the order. The shelter also referred her to the Nita City office of Nita Legal Services. An attorney from Nita Legal Services helped her file for divorce and is representing her in the hearing on a permanent injunction.

The following witnesses are available to be called:

1. Sara Cooper
2. Marcus Horton
3. Jacob Cooper
4. Debra Scott

The parties have stipulated that if called to testify, Officer Gunther Toody's testimony would be consistent with the information in his report.

The case file uses the following form for all dates:

This year (the year in which the case is being tried)	YR-0
Month of the trial	Month-0
Month preceding trial	Month-1
Two months ago	Month-2
Last year	YR-1
The year before last	YR-2

And so on.

In working with witnesses and making presentations to the court, kindly use the actual year in place of the shorthand YR-1, etc.

This problem was written to honor all of the wonderful lawyers, judges, and law teachers who volunteer their time and expertise to teach at programs for lawyers representing under-served communities. These people give their hearts and souls to help improve the practice of law. They prove we are still a profession that seeks to ensure the rule of law is applied everywhere and for every person.

Witness Statements

Statement of Marcus Horton

My name is Marcus Horton. I'm seventeen years old and live here in Nita City with my family. I attend Roosevelt School for the Sciences and am an honors student. I have a part-time job at the Yankee Doodle Restaurant at 5th and Main Streets in Nita City. I usually work the early morning shift so I can go to classes when I finish my shift.

The Yankee Doodle Restaurant where I work is right in the middle of the downtown business district in Nita City. The restaurant is always really busy in the morning as people going to work stop for a quick bite to eat or a cup of our famous coffee. The restaurant is located on the main floor of a big office tower. Our space is about 100 feet wide by 300 hundred feet deep. The back part of the restaurant is devoted to the kitchen and the counter where we sell and serve our food. The front of the restaurant has an area where people can stand in line to place their orders, and has tables around the sides. When the restaurant gets busy the lines of customers stretch between the tables at the front of the restaurant back towards the entrance.

My job isn't very challenging but it helps me put away money for college. I want to be an engineer and really love math. Usually I do math problems in my head when I'm working the front counter. Things like trying to figure out statistical averages of what percentage of people like plain coffee versus those who purchase our special latté or the iced mocha frappe. I'm usually pretty good at working word problems while I take and process orders. I rarely get an order wrong even though I'm working a problem in my head and performing other tasks related to my job. Sometimes it does affect how I deal with customers. When it does my boss says something to me. Usually he jokes about it and says to quit being such an "egghead."

I was working on the morning of the 6th day of Month-4. It was a really busy morning and we had been going pretty much nonstop since I started my shift at 5:30 am. I had a big test in world history that day so I had stayed up late to study. I was pretty tired when I started work but the crowd got me going. Even though I had a test that afternoon I was working a calculus problem in my head that day.

I remember the couple really well. I took their order. She had our Special Oatmeal Breakfast with extra fruit and he had the Super Dooper Pancake meal. The reason I remember them is he was wearing one of those ridiculous t-shirts that said, "I'm with Stupid" and hers said "Me too." They were arguing when I took their order and both smelled of alcohol. Just because I go to the "brainiak" school doesn't mean I don't know how alcohol smells. They continued to bicker while I got their order. When I served them they went and sat down at a table on the far right side of the restaurant from where I was standing. I went back to taking care of the big line waiting at my register.

About ten minutes later I heard someone shouting over the noise of the crowd. It was coming from over on my right side. I looked over and saw the guy wearing the "I'm with Stupid" shirt stand up and smack the woman he was with in the face. It looked like he hit her really hard and it knocked her off her chair and onto the floor. Luckily, there were two cops sitting at a table to my left. Officers Toody and Muldoon, two regulars at the restaurant, were there having their morning break. I ran over and told them what I saw. They went over to the couple and started talking to them. I'm not sure exactly what happened but the officers put both of them in handcuffs and left the restaurant. The next day I asked the officers what happened. Officer Toody told me they suspected it was domestic violence but they didn't know who started the fight. Since both the man and woman were drunk, they were both arrested for public intoxication. Officer Toody told me I might have to be a witness.

I haven't seen either of the two who were in the fight since that day. The lawyer for the woman asked me to tell you what I saw.

Signed,

Marcus Horton

Marcus Horton
29th day of Month-1

Statement of Sara Cooper

My name is Sara Cooper. I'm now twenty years old. I have been married to Jake for about two years. I married Jake while I was still in high school, when I got pregnant. I miscarried because the doctors said I was drinking too much. I dropped out of high school and for the first year we lived with Jacob's parents. Up until when I went to the woman's shelter we were living together in subsidized public housing. We also received assistance in the form of food stamps. I want to divorce Jake so I can get a new start on life.

I met Jake during my junior year of high school. He had already graduated and was working at the Nita Cannery. He had that bad boy image and lots of girls though Jacob was really hot. He was the first boy I knew who had lots of tattoos and piercings. I felt really lucky that Jake noticed me and liked me. He took me out to some really great places and we partied all the time. We would go to lots of parties and drink until we passed out. During those days Jake seemed to have lots of money that we could spend on having a good time. When I got pregnant I told him he had to make things right by me and my family.

Things really changed after we got married. Jake's bad boy image came true as he started yelling at me all the time. He called me names and told me I was lazy. Living at his parent's house didn't make things any easier. His parents are not very nice people. They fight all the time and Jake's dad hits his mom and swears at her. I guess Jake learned how to treat women from his father. One night after the police came and took Jake's dad to jail for hitting his mother I told Jake we had to move out. He told me we couldn't afford to move anywhere and I told him I would leave if he didn't find another place for us.

Jake doesn't make much money at his job. He did find us a place at Nita Gardens, the public housing apartments for Nita City. He also got us on public assistance so we could receive food stamps. The place is OK and we finally had a place of our own. We don't have much money. I would use some of Jake's salary to buy liquor and use the food stamps for things to eat. I can't cook much so we eat lots of canned stuff, macaroni and cheese, and Ramen.

Jake sometimes comes home late from his job. I can smell when he has been out drinking with his pals. I get upset because I have to stay home and can't join him to party after he gets off work. We get into lots of fights about money and him coming home late. Jacob started acting like his father. He would yell at me and eventually he sometimes would grab me and either push me around or hit me. He never hit me hard enough to leave a mark. I didn't know what to do. My parents abandoned me when I got pregnant. My girl friends from school pretty much drifted away after I got married. Last July Jake went too far and I called the cops on him. They came to the apartment but did not arrest him. They told him to go cool off and he went to his parent's house for the day. Things were better after that– at least for a while.

I eventually found a job at the Food Pantry grocery. I worked the late night shift stocking shelves. The money was OK. Because Jake never shared his money with me for anything other than groceries, I used my salary for my own things: clothes, smokes, and whiskey. Since I didn't have other friends I would stop and buy a bottle when I finished my work shift at 7:00 am. I would go home and drink all day. I would drink until I passed out. When I woke up it was usually time to go to work. After a while I started getting to work late. They didn't like that at the store and the manager fired me.

Because I wasn't bringing in money, and therefore wasn't drinking as much, Jake and I started to go out more. Jake's work shift gives him Thursday and Friday off for his weekend. On the evening of the 5th day of Month-4 I told Jake we should go out and party. He was in a good mood and had won some extra money over a bet. We went over to one of his friend's houses. We really had a good time. There was plenty to drink. Jacob and I danced and talked and had a lot of fun. The party lasted all night. Jake and I were pretty drunk. We both had the "munchies" so we decided to go to the Yankee Doodle fast food restaurant downtown. It's not far from our apartment and we were able to walk there from the party. It was about 7:00 in the morning when we got to the restaurant. During our walk I started to ask Jake why he had been flirting with some of the other girls at the party. That put him in a bad mood. He then got on my case about losing my job and not bringing any money to the marriage. Things went back and forth as we stood in line. I ordered my favorite, some oatmeal with extra fruit. Jake wanted pancakes. We got our order and went and sat down. Even as we ate we continued to fight. I must have said something pretty ugly because Jake got that look in his eyes– the same one his father got when he would hit his wife. Jake called me a drunken slut and I lost it. I threw my oatmeal at him. I think I missed him. Then I picked up the napkin holder to throw. Jake stood up and smacked me across the face. He really clocked me good because it knocked me out of my chair. At that point a couple of cops came over and broke things up. I told them Jake was hitting me. He told them I started it by throwing things at him. The cops couldn't decide if it was abuse so they arrested both of us for public intoxication. They took us to the police station and kept us locked up until we were sober. It was at that point I knew I had to get away from Jake. They released me first and I immediately went to the Nita Battered Women's Shelter.

At the shelter they were really nice to me. They told me I could stay there until I found a place of my own. They helped me fill out the forms to get a court order to keep Jake away from me. They even went with me to the courts to get the order. They also got me to go to the Legal Aid office to get a divorce and to make the court order permanent. One of the counselors at the shelter convinced me to go to Alcoholics Anonymous. I've been sober since then. I also was able to get another job stocking shelves. I know now I made a big mistake in marrying Jake. I want out of the marriage and want to go back to school and get my life back.

Signed,

Sarah Cooper

Sara Cooper
27th day of Month-1

Statement of Debra Scott

My name is Debra Scott. I'm married with five children. I live in the suburbs of Nita City with my family. I work in downtown Nita City in the marketing department of Nita Furniture Warehouse. Our department is responsible for radio, television, print, and electronic advertising for the company. We have stores all over the state of Nita and in the surrounding four states. You would know our ads as we are the ones who make use of all the cute wild animals. I am one of the copywriters for the department. I love my job and the company. The owner is a good, religious family man.

I was in the Yankee Doodle Restaurant on the morning of the 6th day of Month-4. I stop at the Yankee Doodle every morning to get one of their yummy vanilla cappuccinos and a sweet roll. It gives me a few minutes of quiet time to get myself ready for a very busy and hectic work day. We are always under a great deal of pressure to produce copy and increase sales for the company. The restaurant was very busy that day and it was hard to find a spot to sit quietly and enjoy my drink. I was also trying to read my emails on my tablet. I was having trouble concentrating because of the noise.

I was trying to read a cute message from one of my friends from church when this really scruffy couple sat down at the table right behind me. I could tell they had been drinking because they really smelled of alcohol when they walked past me. I don't drink myself and I certainly could not understand how they could be intoxicated at such an early hour on a work day. They were bickering with each other as they went to sit down and I thought to myself that I would have to move or leave sooner than I had planned. It annoyed me that they were interrupting my one moment of peace before I started work.

I decided I would take my drink and go to the office because they were getting louder and louder. The next thing I knew the woman in the shirt that said "Me too" called the man "Asshole" and threw her bowl at him. He ducked but the food still hit him and then got all over me as well. I had oatmeal on my suit and my tablet. First he said something like, "Calm down Sara." When she started to pick up something else to throw he stood up, called her an ugly name, and slapped her across the face. You could tell she was really drunk because she lost her balance and fell out of her chair. I don't think he hit her very hard. She certainly deserved what she got. I had to take my suit to the cleaners and the suede cover to my tablet now has stains on it.

Right then two police officers came over and separated the two. They took each of them aside—one with each officer—and started talking with them. I decided to wait to see what would happen. It ended up the cops put both of them in handcuffs. I went up to the really tall officer, the one named Muldoon, and told him I saw everything and said it was self defense by the man. He was very courteous and took my name and phone number. I guess that's why you are talking to me today. I asked him why they were arresting the man and he told me they could not tell what had actually happened so they were arresting both for public intoxication.

I understand the woman is trying to get some type of protective order against the man. That's not right, as she was the one who started things. I do not want to get involved but I think it would be a shame if he was blamed for something she started.

Signed,

Debra Scott

Debra Scott
28th day of Month-1

Statement of Jacob Cooper

My name is Jacob Cooper. Lots of people call me Jake. I'm twenty-two years old. I live at Nita Gardens Apartments, 874 Jackson Avenue, Nita City. At least I do for now. They just gave me a notice of eviction because I have allegedly abused my wife. I am married but my wife, Sara, is not living with me right now. I do not know where she is living because it is some woman's shelter and I can't find out the address.

We have been married since June of YR-2. Sara forced me to marry her because she was pregnant. I was pretty upset at the time but since then I've come to really love her. I'm so sorry that all this has happened. I want her to come home and promise I will work hard to change my life. All this is the worst thing that has ever happened to me. Last July the police gave me a card about anger management courses and once I get this mess straightened out I plan to attend those classes. I know now how wrong I was in hitting Sara.

I work at the Nita Cannery on the assembly line. I make minimum wage but it is steady work. I never finished high school so I do not have a lot of choice about jobs. Sara does not work so we live hand to mouth. We don't have any health insurance or other benefits. Because we have so little money we get subsidized housing and food stamps. It has been hard to make ends meet. This is especially true because Sara uses some of our money to buy booze. I have been trying to get her to quit drinking and realize she has a problem. She ignores me and keeps on getting drunk. Maybe this mess will help her understand she shouldn't drink and should get some help.

When we first got married we lived with my parents. Sara never liked my folks and was always trying to get me to agree to move out. Once when my parents had a big fight the cops came to the house. Sara told me she wouldn't live in the same place as a man who hit his woman. I didn't know what else to do so I went out and applied for public assistance. I was relieved when we got support for an apartment in Nita Gardens. Sara was really happy to have a place of our own. Just the same it really stretched our dollars to the limits.

Things were pretty happy when we first moved. Sara was happy playing house and having a place of our own. After awhile she started to complain that we weren't partying as much. I told her we didn't have the money to buy drinks but that didn't satisfy her. She really started to nag me about the fact she wasn't having any fun anymore. I admit this would make me mad and we would fight about it. When my parents would fight my father would always control things by yelling at my mom. If she really got out of control he would smack her. That usually settled things down and things would get better. I figured if yelling worked for my father it should work for me. One day in July of YR-1 Sara really pushed my buttons about not having enough money. I lost it and did what my dad would do, I yelled at Sara. When she yelled even louder I smacked her. Her reaction was not like my mom, she immediately called the police. I had not hit her very hard and when they arrived they took me outside and told me if they ever had to come back I was going straight to jail. The officer gave me a card about anger management and told me to look into classes. He said if I didn't learn to control my temper it would only lead to bad things. I guess he was right.

The next day I told Sara that if she wanted to party so much she had to get a job so we had more money. She went out and got a job stocking shelves at night at the local grocery store. I never saw any of her wages as she would spend it on things for herself– new clothes, make-up, and other girl stuff. I did notice there would be empty liquor bottles around the house. I never had any but the bottles would pile up and Sara would often be passed out drunk when I came home from work. She would wake up, eat something, and go to work. My life was pretty miserable. I never saw Sara, except for when she was passed out sleeping. I figured I needed to have some fun as well. While Sara would work I would go out with friends from work. Mostly we would have a couple of beers, play a little pool or poker, and just have some laughs.

Things changed again in Month-6, when Sara got fired from her job. She told me they had let her go because she was always late for work. I think it was also because she was usually drunk. I told Sara she really needed to cut down on the booze. That only started another fight so I dropped the subject. Because we didn't have the money it slowed down her drinking.

On the 5th day of Month-4 I won a bunch of money at a poker game. It was enough for us to go out and have a good time. I didn't have to work the next two days so I told Sara we would go party at a friend's house. We really did party– all night. It was a great time and it was like the good old days between us. We left the party at around 6:00 am. We were walking because we were both really toasted. Sara had the munchies so we decided to stop at the Yankee Doodle to get some breakfast. We arrived around 7:00 and stood in line to place our order. While we were in line Sara started to get on my case about making more money so we could party all the time. Then she was angry because she said I had been flirting with girls at the party. We got our food and went and sat down. Sara kept bugging me about making more money so she could have a better time with her life. I finally had enough and told her she was a drunk and needed to get a job so we could afford things in life. She started yelling at me, telling me I didn't run her life. I told her to shut up and she really got mad. That's when she threw her bowl of oatmeal at me. I ducked so most of the oatmeal missed me. It hit the lady sitting behind me. I told her to calm down and that we would get in trouble. Then she started to pick up the napkin holder to throw. I thought she would really throw it and I should defend myself. I stood up and tried to knock the napkin holder out of her hand. I missed and hit Sara across the face with my hand. She was so drunk she lost her balance and fell off her chair. I just stood there staring at her.

Two cops came over to the table at that point. I have no idea where they came from but knew I was probably in big trouble. They helped Sara up and each took one of us aside to hear what we had to say. I told the officer what had happened and apologized for hitting Sara. He told me he thought I should go to jail for domestic violence. I was really scared at that point. The other cop came back with Sara and the two cops talked. We both stood there while the police talked with the woman who Sara hit with her oatmeal and some kid from behind the counter. The cop named Toody told me they couldn't decide who had assaulted whom and would not charge either of us with domestic violence. He did say we were publicly drunk and we would go to the station to sober up. They took us to the police station and that was the last time I saw Sara.

The next thing I knew I got these legal papers saying I had to stay away from Sara. They also said I had to come back for a hearing to decide if I had to stay away from her forever. I also got some other papers from some lawyer saying Sara was divorcing me. I don't want that to happen. I love her and will promise to change and control my temper if she comes home. I want her to be happy and get sober. I'm just really sorry this whole thing ever happened.

The things that Sara said in the papers she used to get that restraining order thing are a big bunch of crap. She blows everything up. Except for my hitting her in the Yankee Doodle I have not hit Sara since the cops came in July, YR-1. She starts most of the fights because she is drunk. When she is drunk she gets really mean. She's the one who starts the fights and yells all the time. She claims I push her. I do, but it is after she starts pushing me. It isn't some playful push either – she really gives me a shove. I admit I yell back after she starts screaming at me. She knows how to push my buttons and says things she knows will make me angry. I don't threaten her about money. The truth is we don't have enough to pay our bills and let her drink. Where the stories she is telling came from I don't know. I think they must be suggesting she say these things at that women's shelter. It's just not really true. If I could see Sara I know we could work things out. I still love her and really want to have things work out between us.

Signed,

Jacob Cooper

Jacob Cooper
5th day of Month-1

EXHIBITS

Exhibit 1

NITA POLICE DEPARTMENT
INCIDENT REPORT

Complainant: Marcus Horton
Accused: Jacob Cooper (DOB: 8/14/YR-22) and Sara Cooper (DOB: 2/23/YR-19)
Location: Yankee Doodle Restaurant, 5th & Main, Nita City
Nature of Call: Domestic Violence and Public Drunkenness
Date: 6th day of MONTH-4
Date of Report: 7th day of Month-4
By: Gunther Toody

On scene having breakfast break when alerted to altercation by complaining witness. Time: 7:25 a.m.

OBSERVATIONS

Partner Francis Muldoon and this officer were on break at the Yankee Doodle Restaurant located at 5th and Main Streets when the counter employee directed our attention to a disturbance occurring in the eating area of the restaurant. Identified a woman sitting on the floor and a male standing over the woman. Partner and I approached the two. I could smell alcohol emanating from both parties. Counter employee stated the man hit the woman across the face with his hand. Man was wearing blue jeans and a t-shirt reading, "I'm with Stupid." Woman was dressed similarly, in jeans and a shirt reading, "Me too." Man identified as Jacob Cooper. Woman identified as Sara Cooper. Both of 874 Jackson Avenue, Apartment 216 W, Nita City.

SPONTANEOUS UTTERANCE

Before I could ask what happened, male subject Jacob Cooper stated, "She started it. She makes me crazy, that drunken bitch. She started throwing things at me and I defended myself."

APPEARANCE/DEMEANOR

As Cooper was speaking to me, he stated that he was going to get the blame for this. Cooper appeared tense and nervous throughout the utterance. Subject is approximately six feet tall, weighing 180–190 pounds.

INJURIES

Jacob Cooper had no visible injuries nor did he complain of any. Sara Cooper had no visible signs of injury. There were no red marks or bruises on her face or those portions of her body this officer could observe.

OBSERVATIONS

Cooper was clearly agitated. He had wet stains on his right shoulder, conforming with his statement that oatmeal had been thrown on him. Mrs. Cooper continued to sit on the floor. She showed no signs of being injured and was not crying. There were no red marks or evidence of bruising on her face. She did appear to be angry. Based on observations and what subject Jacob Cooper stated, I separated the couple and Officer Muldoon and I each spoke with one of the parties to gather facts. I then continued my conversation with Mr. Cooper. Officer Muldoon spoke with Mrs. Cooper.

STATEMENT: COOPER, SARA

Sara Cooper, who appeared to have been drinking but was coherent, related she and her husband were arguing at the restaurant. Mrs. Cooper indicated her husband was verbally abusing her and threatened her physically. She retaliated by throwing a bowl of oatmeal at her husband and was attempting to throw the napkin holder at him. At this point he stood and struck her across the face with the flat of his hand, knocking her to the floor. Mrs. Cooper was crying and said she thought her husband was really going to hurt her. She was visibly shaken, and because of her inebriation or anxiety was unable to say more. She did admit that she had been drinking heavily for the past ten hours.

COMPLAINING WITNESS STATEMENT

Marcus Horton, a counter clerk at the Yankee Doodle Restaurant, was the person who initially alerted this officer to the situation. At approximately 7:30 am Horton came up to this officer and announced he had just witnessed a diner hit another person. He pointed to the parties and told my partner and me that he heard loud, angry voices coming from the right side of the restaurant. When he looked over to see the reason for the raised voices he observed a man, later identified as Jacob Cooper, stand and strike the woman sitting across from him across the face. The person who he struck had fallen to the floor as a result of the blow. Horton advised us that he had served the couple and they had been arguing with each other in line and as they placed their orders. Horton also indicated both had an odor of alcohol about them.

OTHER WITNESS STATEMENT

Debra Scott, a diner, made herself know to this officer and indicated she observed the altercation. Mrs. Scott observed the two parties and as they sat at the table directly across from her. She indicated they were arguing as they ate their meal and their voices gradually increased in volume. At one point Mrs. Cooper called her husband an "asshole" and then threw her meal at her husband. The thrown bowl of food spilled on both Mr. Cooper and Mrs. Scott. Mrs. Scott declined to press charges against Mrs. Cooper but was willing to testify. After he was hit with food Mr. Cooper said to his wife, "Calm down." She continued to yell and appeared to be getting ready to throw another object. Mr. Cooper then stood and slapped his wife across the face. Scott testifies that following the contact Mrs. Cooper lost her balance and fell to the floor. Scott further testifies that both parties were very drunk and she believes Mrs. Cooper fell as a result of her drunken state rather than because she had been slapped.

ARREST MADE

On the 6th day of Month-4 at 7:45 a.m., Jacob and Sara Cooper were placed under arrest for public intoxication. Neither was handcuffed. Miranda rights read as per card, both refused to speak further. No further conversation with parties.

INTOXILYZER RESULTS

At about 8:45 a.m. DUI technician McHugh intoxilyzed both parties in my presence with the result being a .123% blood alcohol content for Mr. Cooper and a .185% blood alcohol for Mrs. Cooper. Refer to intoxilyzer report for all pertinent information.

Exhibit 2

Case Name Cooper v Cooper Case Number: CR765

Information Sheet for Registering a Protection Order

Complete this form and attach it to the Verified Complaint for Protection Order Form JDF 402.

> If this form is incomplete, information may not be posted at Nita Bureau of Investigation (NBI) for Law Enforcement officials to access and your protection order may not be properly enforced.

Information about You (The Protected Party)

Full Name: **Sara Jane Cooper** Date of Birth: **2/23/YR-20**
Physical description Gender: □ Male ■ Female Race: **Caucasian**
Height: **5′ 3″** Weight: **145** Hair Color: **Brown** Eye Color: **Brown**
Complete Home Address: **874 Jackson Avenue** Apartment #: **216 W**
City: **Nita City** State: **Nita**
Telephone #s: Home: Work: Cell: **555-720-6494**

Identify relationship between you and the Restrained Party:

Spouse Former Spouse Both parties are parents of the child(ren)
Current co-habitants Former Co-habitants Restrained Party is a parent of the child(ren)
Parties have been or are involved in an intimate relationship for ______ months.

Other persons to be protected: (i.e. children)

Full name of Protected Party	Sex	Race	Date of Birth

Information about Party to be Restrained

Full Name: **Jacob Marley Cooper** Date of Birth: **8/14/YR-22**
Physical description: Gender: ■ Male □ Female Race: **Caucasian**
Height: 5′ 11″ Weight: **185** Hair Color: **Brown** Eye Color: **Hazel**
Complete Home Address: 874 Jackson Avenue Apartment #: 216 W
City: **Nita City** State: **Nita**
Telephone #s: Home: Work: Cell: **555-720-7549**

Date: **8th Day of Month-4** **Signature:** *Sarah Cooper*

<table>
<tr><td>□ Municipal Court □ County Court ■ District Court □ Juvenile Court

Darrow County, Nita</td><td rowspan="2">Court Use Only</td></tr>
<tr><td>Plaintiff/Petitioner: Sara Jane Cooper
Date of Birth: 2/23/YR-20
v.
Defendant/Respondent: Jacob M. Cooper
Date of Birth: 8/14/YR-22</td></tr>
<tr><td>Attorney or Party Without Attorney (Name and Address)

Sara Jane Cooper
Nita City Battered Women's Shelter

Phone: 444-720-6494
The address of the Protected Person may be omitted from the written order of the Court, including the Register of actions</td><td>Case Number: CR765

Division______ Courtroom ______</td></tr>
</table>

VERIFIED □ COMPLAINT ■ MOTION FOR CIVIL PROTECTION ORDER

I, Sara Jane Cooper, (name of person) request this Court to issue a Civil Protection Order, and in support of this request state the following:

1. I am seeking this Civil Protection Order as a victim of the following: (Mark the applicable circumstances.)

■ Domestic violence (§ 13-14-101(2), N.R.S.
□ Stalking (§ 18-3-602, N.R.S.)
□ Sexual Assault (§ 18-3-402(1), N.R.S.)
□ Unlawful Sexual Contact (§ 18-3-404, N.R.S.)
□ Physical Assault, Threat, or other situation.

2. I reside or am employed in the County of Darrow, State of Nita, and I, Sara Cooper (name of person) resides or is employed in the County of Darrow, State of Nita. I know Sara Cooper (name of person) because: it is myself.

3. The other Protected Persons are (list full name, date of birth, sex, and race):

Full Name of Protected Person	Date of Birth	Sex	Race

□ I have completed and attached the form titled "Affidavit Regarding Children" JDF 404 as children are identified as Protected Persons above.

4. a) The most recent incident that causes me to ask for a Civil Protection Order occurred on or about 6th Day of MONTH-4, at about 7:30 a.m., in Darrow County, when Jacob Cooper (name of person) did the following to me and/or the above named Protected Persons: *Be specific: What was the threat or acts of violence? Where did this occur? Were the minor children or other Protected Persons present? Was a weapon involved?*

We were in the Yankee Doodle Restaurant on the 6th day of MONTH- 4, when Jacob started cursing and threatening me. He then slapped me across the face and knocked me to the floor. I am concerned he will continue to hit me and verbally abuse me. We have no children and there were no weapons involved.

b) The most serious incident that causes me to ask for a Civil Protection Order occurred on or about July 8, YR-1 at about 4:00 pm in Darrow (County), when Jacob Cooper did the following to me and/or the above named Protected Persons. *Be specific: What was the threat or acts of violence? Where did this occur? Were the minor children or other Protected Persons present? Was a weapon involved?*

After we moved into our apartment in Nita Gardens, Jacob started to verbally abuse me by yelling at me and pushing me around. On July 8th, YR-1 Jacob and I were at our apartment in Nita Gardens when he started to curse at me. He then started to push me and knocked me down. He hit me several times on the face and in the stomach. I was really hurt and very scared. I called the police. Since that time he has threatened to not give me any money and to send me back to my parents' house if I didn't behave like a "good wife."

c) Are you aware of any other Protection Orders currently in effect against you or the other person? □ yes ■ No If YES, list any relevant information, such as the issuing Court, State, and date of the order:

5. I believe that I and/or the other Protected Persons named in this action are in imminent danger from Jacob Cooper (name of person):

■ Harm to my/our life if he/she is not restrained as requested.

■ Physical or emotional harm to my/our emotional health or welfare if he/she is not excluded from the family home or the home of another.

6. ■ I request that I be permitted to omit my address from this Verified Complaint/Motion for Civil Protection Order, because I fear that including my address will endanger me and/or the other Protected Persons.

7. I request the following relief from the Court that Jacob Cooper (name of person):

a) ■ Be ordered to refrain from attacking, beating, molesting, intimidating, and verbally harassing me, following me, threatening my life, or threatening me with serious bodily injury.

b) ■ Be ordered to have <u>no contact</u> at all with me or the other Protected Persons.

or

□ Be allowed only the following limited contact with me or the other Protected Persons: *Be specific:*

c) ■ Be excluded from my home at (address): If you checked section 6, do not provide your address.

d) □ Be ordered to have no contact with the minor children and that I be awarded temporary care and control and interim decision-making responsibilities for the children

e) □ Be ordered to restrain from threatening, molesting, injuring, killing, taking, transferring, encumbering, concealing, or disposing of an animal owned, possessed, leased, kept, or held by me or my minor child(ren), or other protected persons. Arrangements for possession and care are as follows:

f) □ Other

I swear or affirm under penalty of perjury that the information contained in this Verified Complaint/Motion for Civil Protection Order is true and correct. I understand that once a Civil Protection Order is issued it cannot be modified or dismissed by me or the other person without permission of the Court.

Sarah Jane Cooper

____
Attorney, if applicable
Address and Telephone number:

■ Plaintiff/Petitioner □ Defendant/Respondent

STOP: If you checked box number 6, do not fill in your address and telephone number.

Subscribed and affirmed, or sworn to before me, in the County of Darrow, State of Nita

this 8th day of Month-4.

My Commission Expires: 31 October, YR+1

Victoria Schultz

Notice: Nita Revised Statutes § 13 - 14-102 identifies that a temporary injunction may be issued by the Court and that upon personal service or upon waiver and acceptance of service by the Restrained Person, is to be in effect against the Restrained Person for a period determined to be appropriate by the Court. This injunction restrains the Restrained Person from:

1.Ceasing to make payments for mortgage or rent, insurance, utilities or related services, transportation, medical care, or child care when the Restrained Person has a prior existing duty or legal obligation for making such payments.

2.Transferring, encumbering, concealing, or in any way disposing of personal effects or real property, except in the usual course of business or for the necessities of life.

Exhibit 3

Yankee Doodle Restaurant
5th & Main, Nita City
As it appeared on 6th day of Month-4

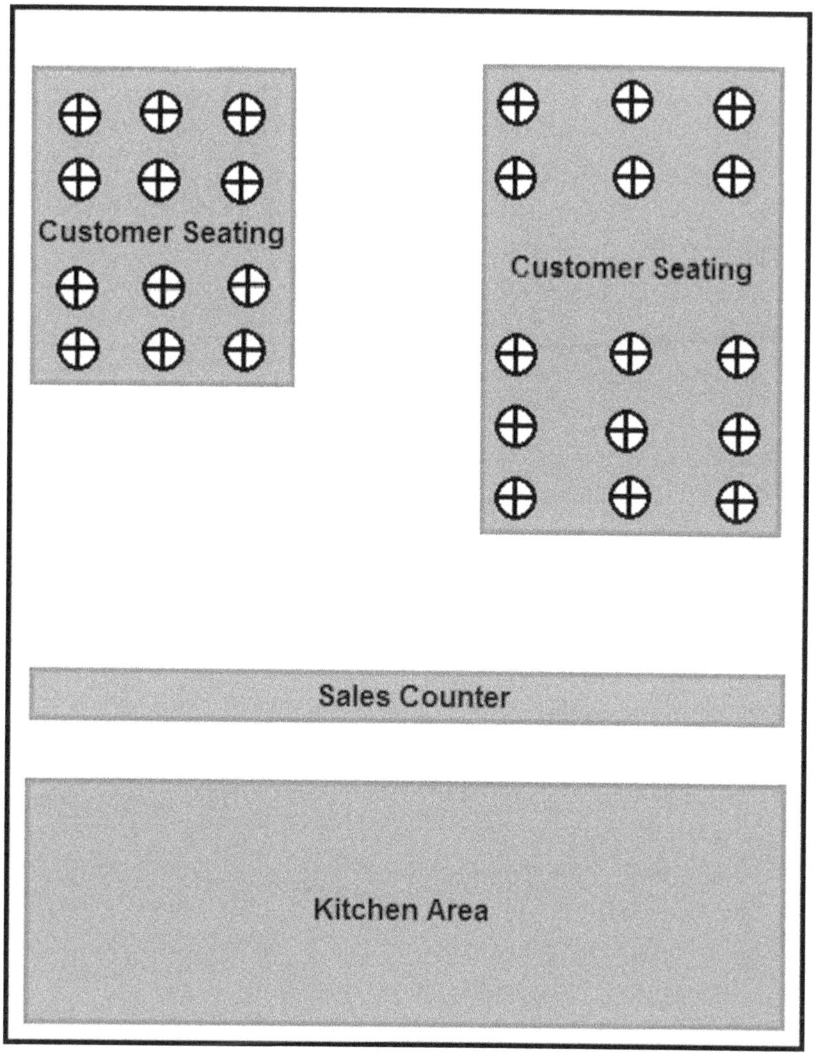

Exhibit 4

Yankee Doodle Restaurant
5th & Main, Nita City
As it appeared on 6th day of Month-4

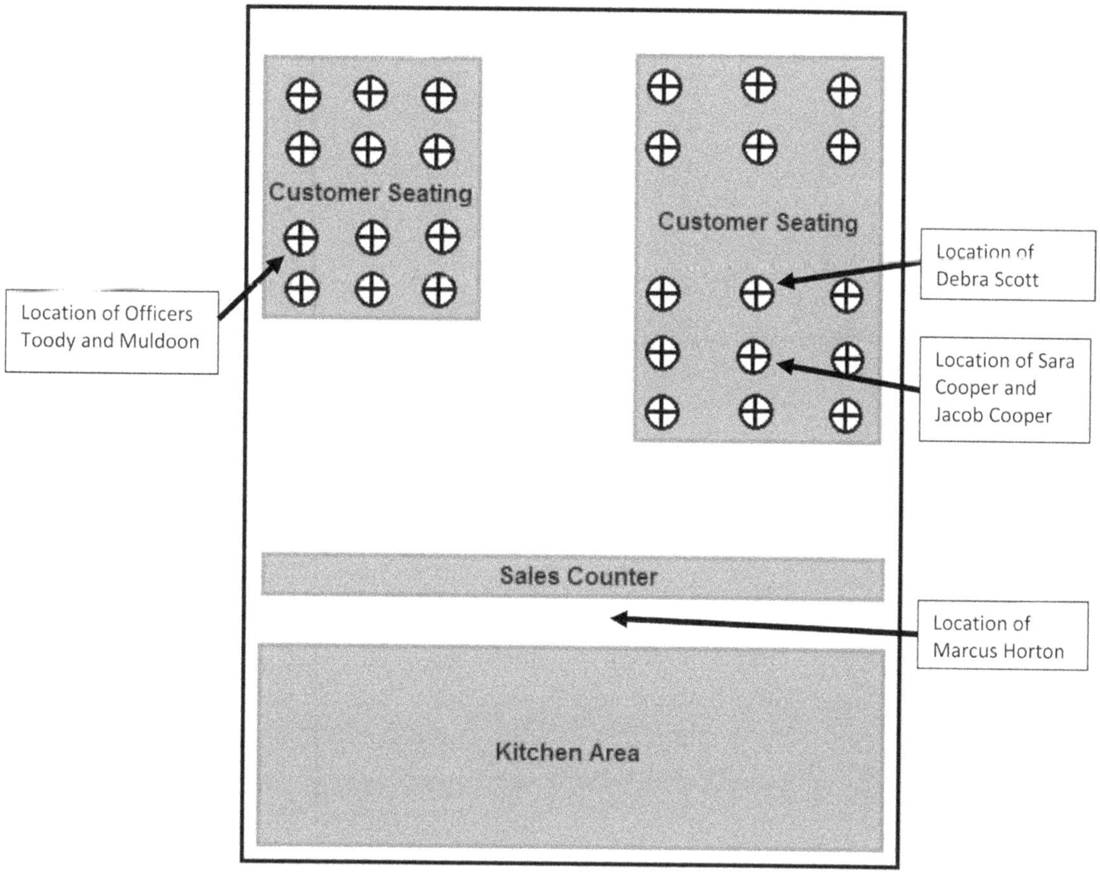

Exhibit 5

Interior view of customer seating area of Yankee Doodle Restaurant

Exhibit 6

SALES COUNTER AND KITCHEN AREA OF YANKEE DOODLE RESTAURANT

Exhibit 7

Arrest photograph of Jacob Cooper
taken on the 6th day of Month-4

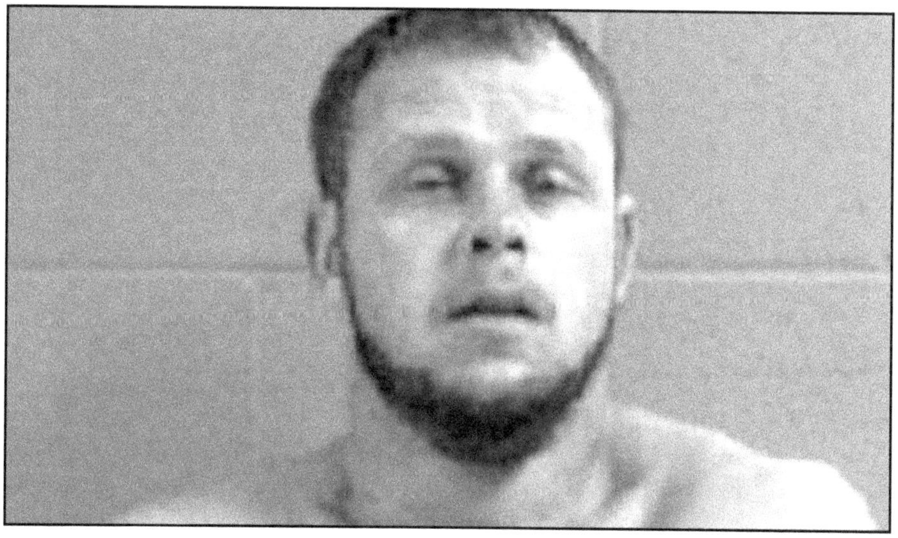

Jacob Cooper

Exhibit 8

Arrest photograph of Sarah Cooper
taken on the 6th day of Month-4

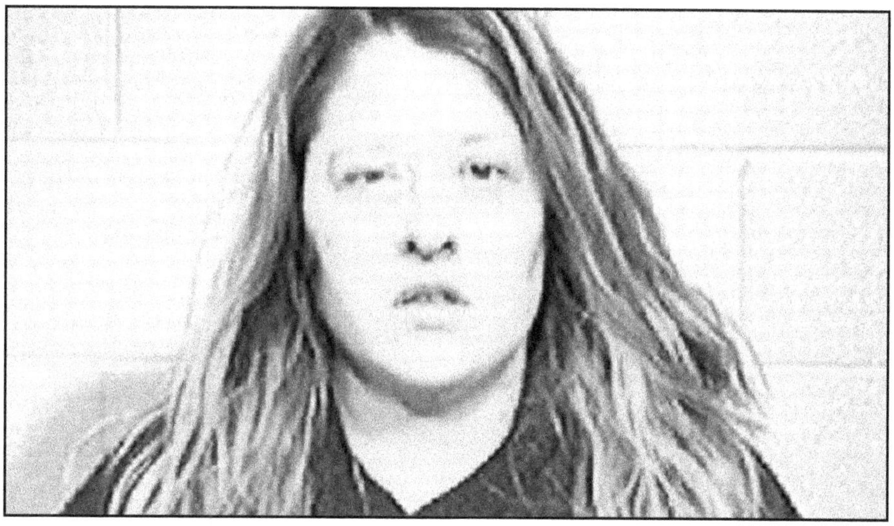

Sara Cooper

STATUTES

18-6-800.3. Definitions.

As used in this part 8, unless the context otherwise requires:

(1) "Domestic violence" means an act or threatened act of violence upon a person with whom the actor is or has been involved in an intimate relationship. "Domestic violence" also includes any other crime against a person, or against property, including an animal, or any municipal ordinance violation against a person, or against property, including an animal, when used as a method of coercion, control, punishment, intimidation, or revenge directed against a person with whom the actor is or has been involved in an intimate relationship.

(2) "Intimate relationship" means a relationship between spouses, former spouses, past or present unmarried couples, or persons who are both the parents of the same child regardless of whether the persons have been married or have lived together at any time.

13-14-102. Civil protection orders - legislative declaration.

(1) (a) The general assembly hereby finds that the issuance and enforcement of protection orders are of paramount importance in the state of Nita because protection orders promote safety, reduce violence, and prevent serious harm and death. In order to improve the public's access to protection orders and to assure careful judicial consideration of requests and effective law enforcement, there shall be two processes for obtaining protection orders within the state of Nita: a simplified civil process and a mandatory criminal process.

(b) The general assembly further finds and declares that:

(I) Domestic violence is not limited to physical threats of violence and harm but includes financial control, document control, property control, and other types of control that make a victim more likely to return to an abuser due to fear of retaliation or inability to meet basic needs;

(II) Victims of domestic violence in many cases are unable to access resources to seek lasting safety options;

(III) These victims need the assistance of additional court orders to meet their immediate needs for food, shelter, transportation, medical care, and child care at the time they go to court for a civil protection order; and

(IV) These additional court orders are needed not only in cases that end in dissolution of marriage but also in cases in which reconciliation is appropriate, as well as in other cases.

(1.5) Any municipal court of record, if authorized by the municipal governing body; any county court; and any district, probate, or juvenile court shall have original concurrent jurisdiction to issue a temporary or permanent civil protection order against an adult or against a juvenile who is ten years of age or older for any of the following purposes:

(a) To prevent assaults and threatened bodily harm;
(b) To prevent domestic violence;
(c) To prevent emotional abuse of the elderly or of an at-risk adult;

or

(d) To prevent stalking.

(2) Any civil protection order issued pursuant to this section shall be issued using the standardized set of forms developed by the state court administrator pursuant to section 13-1-136

(2.5) Venue for filing a motion or complaint pursuant to this section is proper in any county where the acts that are the subject of the motion or complaint occur, in any county where one of the parties resides, or in any county where one of the parties is employed. This requirement for venue does not prohibit the change of venue to any other county appropriate under applicable law.

(3) A motion for a temporary civil protection order shall be set for hearing, which hearing may be ex parte, at the earliest possible time and shall take precedence over all matters, except those matters of the same character that have been on the court docket for a longer period of time. The court shall hear all such motions as expeditiously as possible.

(3.3) Any district court, in an action commenced under the "Uniform Dissolution of Marriage Act," article 10 of title 14, N.R.S., shall have authority to issue temporary and permanent protection orders pursuant to the provisions of subsection 1.5 of this section. Such protection order may be as a part of a motion for a protection order accompanied by an affidavit filed in an action brought under article 10 of title 14, N.R.S. Either party may request the court to issue a protection order consistent with any other provision of this article.

(3.7) At the time a protection order is requested pursuant to this section, the court shall inquire about, and the requesting party and such party's attorney shall have an independent duty to disclose, knowledge such party and such party's attorney may have concerning the existence of any prior protection or restraining order of any court addressing in whole or in part the subject matter of the requested protection order. In the event there are conflicting restraining or protection orders, the court shall consider, as its first priority, issues of public safety. An order that prevents assaults, threats of assault, or other bodily harm shall be given precedence over an order that deals with the disposition of property or other tangible assets. Every effort shall be made by judicial officers to clarify conflicting orders.

(4) (a) A temporary civil protection order may be issued if the issuing judge or magistrate finds that an imminent danger exists to the person or persons seeking protection under the civil protection order. In determining whether an imminent danger exists to the life or health of one or more persons, the court shall consider when the most recent incident of abuse or threat of harm occurred, as well as all other relevant evidence concerning the safety and protection of the persons seeking the protection order. However, the court shall not deny a petitioner the relief requested solely because of a lapse of time between an act of abuse or threat of harm and filing of the petition for a protection order.

(5) Upon the filing of a complaint duly verified, alleging that the defendant has committed acts that would constitute grounds for a civil protection order, any judge or magistrate, after hearing the evidence and being fully satisfied therein that sufficient cause exists, may issue a temporary civil protection order to prevent the actions complained of and a citation directed to the defendant commanding the defendant to appear before the court at a specific time and date and to show cause, if any, why said temporary civil protection order should not be made permanent. In addition, the court may order any other relief that the court deems appropriate. Complaints may be filed by persons seeking protection for themselves or for others as provided in section 26-3.1-102 (1) (b) and (1) (c), N.R.S.

(9) (a) On the return date of the citation, or on the day to which the hearing has been continued, the judge or magistrate shall examine the record and the evidence. If upon such examination the

judge or magistrate is of the opinion that the defendant has committed acts constituting grounds for issuance of a civil protection order and that unless restrained will continue to commit such acts, the judge or magistrate shall order the temporary civil protection order to be made permanent or order a permanent civil protection order with different provisions from the temporary civil protection order. The judge or magistrate shall inform said defendant that a violation of the civil protection order shall constitute a criminal offense pursuant to section 18-6-803.5, N.R.S., or shall constitute contempt of court and subject the defendant to such punishment as may be provided by law. If the defendant fails to appear before the court for the show cause hearing at the time and on the date identified in the citation issued by the court, and the court finds that the defendant was properly served with the temporary protection order and such citation, it shall not be necessary to re-serve the defendant to make the protection order permanent. However, if the court modifies the protection order on the motion of the protected party, the modified protection order shall be served upon the defendant.

(b) Notwithstanding the provisions of paragraph (a) of this subsection (9), the judge or magistrate, after examining the record and the evidence, for good cause shown, may continue the temporary protection order and the show cause hearing to a date certain not to exceed one hundred twenty days after the date of the hearing if he or she determines such continuance would be in the best interests of the parties and if both parties are present at the hearing and agree to the continuance.

18-1-704 Use of physical force in defense of a person

(1) Except as provided in subsections (2) and (3) of this section, a person is justified in using physical force upon another person in order to defend himself or a third person from what he reasonably believes to be the use or imminent use of unlawful physical force by that other person, and he may use a degree of force which he reasonably believes to be necessary for that purpose.

(2) Deadly physical force may be used only if a person reasonably believes a lesser degree of force is inadequate and:

(a) The actor has reasonable ground to believe, and does believe, that he or another person is in imminent danger of being killed or of receiving great bodily injury;

(3) Notwithstanding the provisions of subsection (1) of this section, a person is not justified in using physical force if:

(a) With intent to cause bodily injury or death to another person, he provokes the use of unlawful physical force by that other person.

Cooper v. Cooper is designed to be tried as a bench trial. As such, there are no jury instructions. Those using the file should use the included statutes for their case analysis. In presenting their case advocates should consider that bench trials also must be interesting to the finder of fact (the judge). While opening statement and closing argument may not require the same level of drama as presented to a jury, opening statement must still have a theme and show the wrong done to the party. Likewise, closing argument must outline how the elements were proved, flaws with witnesses, and tell the court what you want to happen. Keep in mind that, like jurors, judges are human and the skills of persuasion still apply.

Suggested Time Guidelines
½ Day Bench Trial

8:00 – 8:10 a.m. (12:30 – 12:40 p.m.)	Opening Statements – 10 minutes Each side 5 minutes
8:10 – 9:20 a.m. (12:40 – 1:50 p.m.)	Plaintiff's Case – 70 minutes (45 direct/25 cross)
9:20 – 9:30 a.m. (1:50 – 2:00 p.m.)	Break – 10 minutes
9:30 – 10:40 a.m. (2:00 – 3:10 p.m.)	Defendant's Case – 70 minutes (45 direct/25 cross)
10:40 – 10:50 a.m. (3:10 – 3:20 p.m.)	Closing Arguments – 10 minutes Each side 5 minutes
10:50 – 11:00 a.m. (3:20 – 3:30 p.m.)	Break – 10 minutes
11:00 – 11:30 a.m. (3:30 – 4:00 p.m.)	Critique – 30 minutes
11:30 a.m. (4:00 p.m.)	Adjourn

Montane v. Hadden

Special thanks to Joel Hayes Jr. for his ideas and comments in creating this case file. Joel's real world experience and knowledge of legal services work provided significant help in drafting the problem. His commitment to public service and educating lawyers is an example to all.

INTRODUCTION

This is an action to terminate a residential lease in a legal services setting. Christine Montane and her sister Josephine Montane seek to terminate their lease agreement based upon the landlord's failure to deal with a bed bug infestation. The sisters assert they provided timely notice to the landlord about the problem and the landlord failed to take appropriate action. Pat Hadden, the landlord, defends by claiming the Montane sisters introduced the bed bugs to the dwelling and then failed to provide him access to remedy the problem. He further asserts he did not receive proper notice of the problem. He seeks to remedy the problem and maintain the existing lease. The Montane sisters are foreign nationals living legally in the United States. They were classified as refugees under U.S. law. The Montane sisters moved to Nita City as part of a relocation plan. Both sisters are currently employed but the younger sister works a part-time job after school. The family lives at the poverty level. English is their second language.

Pretrial discovery has been completed. The applicable law is contained within the file.

All of the witness roles in this case file may be played by either a woman or a man. The facts should be altered to be consistent with witnesses' sex.

The following witnesses are available to be called:

1. Pat Hadden
2. Christine Montane
3. Jan Sommerfeld
4. Joe Santini

The following witness has made a sworn statement but is unavailable for trial. This statement may be used at trial. However, it is subject to any motion brought by the side not wishing to call the witness.

1. Virginia Hoeckle (pronounced Heckle)

The case file uses the following form for all dates:

This year (the year in which the case is being tried)	YR-0
Month of the trial	Month-0
Month preceding trial	Month-1
Two months ago	Month-2
Last year	YR-1
The year before last	YR-2

And so on.

In working with witnesses and making presentations to the court, kindly use the actual year or month in place of the shorthand YR-1, etc.

This problem was written for use at NITA and other public service programs with the intent of helping lawyers and law students improve their trial skills. Focus of the problem is specifically on witness examination skills and storytelling as it relates to presenting factual information to judges and juries.

Please assume all documents were timely filed.

LANDLORD/TENANT COURT, COUNTY OF DARROW, STATE OF NITA

Case No. CR398

SUMMONS FOR TERMINATION OF LEASE

CHRISTINE MONTANE

Plaintiff,

vs.

PAT HADDEN

Defendant.

To the above named Defendant: Take note that

1. On the (Program Date) of Month-0 at 10:00 a.m., in the Nita City Landlord/Tenant Court, 687 Main Street, Nita City, Nita, the Court may be asked to enter judgment against you as set forth in the Complaint.

2. A copy of the Complaint against you is attached.

3. If you do not agree with the Complaint, then you must either:

a. Go to the Court, located at 687 Main Street, Nita City, Nita at the above date and time and file the Answer stating any legal reason you have why judgment should not be entered against you, or

b. File the Answer with the Court before that date and time.

4. When you file your Answer, you must pay a filing fee to the Clerk of the Court.

5. If you file an Answer, you must give or mail a copy to the Plaintiff or the attorney who signed the Complaint.

6. If you do not file with the Court, at or before the time for appearance specified in this Summons, an Answer to the Complaint setting forth the groups upon which you base your claim for possession and denying or admitting all of the material allegations of the Complaint, judgment by default may be taken against you for the possession of the property described in the Complaint; for the rent, if any due or to become due; for present and future damages; and for any other relief to which the Plaintiff is entitled.

7. If you want a jury trial, you must ask for one in the Answer and pay a jury fee in addition to the filing fee.

8. If you want to file an Answer or request a jury trial and you are indigent, you must appear at the above date and time, fill out a financial affidavit, and ask the Court to waive the fees.

Respectfully submitted this 2nd day of Month-2, YR-0.

Nelson Ridgeway

Nelson Ridgeway
Attorney, Nita Legal Services, Inc.

This summons is issued pursuant to Rule 303, Rules of Landlord/Tenant Court Civil Procedure, as amended, and 15-10-231, NRS. A copy of the Complaint must be served with this Summons. This form should be used only for actions filed under Nita's Landlord/Tenant Act. WARNING: All fees are non-refundable. In some cases, a request for a jury trial may be denied pursuant to law even though a jury fee has been paid.

LANDLORD/TENANT COURT, COUNTY OF DARROW, STATE OF NITA

Case No. CR398

VERIFIED COMPLAINT FOR TERMINATION OF LEASE

CHRISTINE MONTANE

Plaintiff,

vs.

PAT HADDEN

Defendant.

COMES NOW, the Plaintiff by and through her attorney, and states as follow:

1. Plaintiff, Christine Montane, is the lessee of the property located at 890 Front Street, Nita City, Nita, the legal description of which is to wit: Lot 4, Baker Subdivision, County of Darrow, Nita City, State of Nita.

2. Plaintiff leased the premises from the Defendant pursuant to a written lease. Rent is due on the first day of each month. Monthly rental of said premises at this time payable by tenant is $1,100.00

4. Plaintiff entered into occupancy of said premises.

5. Plaintiff has been in compliance with all terms of the lease agreement, including payment of rent and maintaining the residence.

6. On approximately the fourth day of Month-3 the Plaintiff discovered the apartment was infested with bed bugs.

7. Plaintiff has made a number requests by telephone and in writing that the Defendant remedy the problem and defendant has failed to resolve the problem.

8. Defendant breached the warranty of habitability for rental agreements as spelled out in NRS 38-12-503 and NRS 38-12-505 by failing to keep the building free of vermin or appropriately exterminate such vermin.

9. Plaintiff has elected to terminate said tenancy on day 31 of Month-1.

10. Plaintiff provided a thirty day written notice to the landlord to either remedy the breach or terminate the rental agreement by surrendering possession of the dwelling unit.

WHEREFORE, Plaintiff prays for termination of lease, present and future damages, attorney fees, costs, and any other relief to which the Plaintiff is entitled.

Dated this 2nd day of Month-2.

CERTIFICATE OF MAILING

I certify that a true copy of the answer was mailed, postage prepaid, to:

Victoria Rogers, JD
Frazier & Dooley
239 Main Street, 4th Fl.
Nita City, Nita

Nelson Ridgeway

Nelson Ridgeway
Attorney, Nita Legal Services, Inc.

Residential Lease Agreement

THIS LEASE AGREEMENT is made and entered into this 28th day of June, YR-1, by and between **Pat Hadden,** hereinafter referred to as "Landlord," and **Christine Montane and Josephine Montane,** hereinafter referred to as "Tenant".

1. Landlord leases to Tenant and Tenant leases from Landlord, upon the terms and conditions contained herein, the dwelling located at **890 Front Street** for the period commencing on the **1st** day of **July, YR-1**, and thereafter until the **31st** day of **July, YR+1**, at which time this Lease Agreement shall automatically renew each year unless terminated in writing. *The Tenant is required to give the Landlord in writing a notice one (1) month (30 days) in advance of his/her moving. Notice must be given on the first day of a month. If notice is given after the first day of the month, the one (1) month (30 day) notice will not start until the following month. (**The notice must be one full calendar month starting on the first day of a month.**)* Rent may be increased at any time after first year and the security deposit cannot be used for rent.
2. Tenant shall pay as rent the sum of $**1,100.00** per month, due and payable monthly, in advance, and no later than 5:00 p.m. by the fourth day of every month. Tenant further agrees to pay a late charge of $**25.00** for each day rent is not received after the fourth day of the month to the Landlord regardless of the cause, including dishonored checks, time being of the essence. An additional Service Charge of $**50.00** will be paid to Landlord for all dishonored checks.
3. As an incentive to Tenant to make rent payments ***before the first of the month*** *and for being responsible for all minor maintenance of the premises*, a pre-payment discount in the amount of $**25.00** may be deducted from the above rental amount each month. **Said discount will be forfeited if Tenant fails to perform as stated above.**
4. Tenant agrees to accept the property in its current condition and to return it in "moving-in clean" condition, or to pay a special cleaning charge of $185.00 upon vacating the premises. The carpets are to be professionally cleaned. If you prefer that we have the carpets cleaned for you the charge will be billed to you. Carpet cleaning costs are in addition to cleaning charge.
5. PETS ARE NOT ALLOWED WITHOUT WRITTEN PERMISSION FROM LANDLORD. As additional rent, Tenant agrees to pay a non-refundable pet fee of $10.00 per month for each pet. All pets on the property not registered under this Lease shall be presumed to be strays and will be disposed of by the appropriate agency as prescribed by law. A Pet Agreement, if applicable, is attached hereto as Exhibit "B", and incorporated herein by reference. PET NAMES AND DESCRIPTION:

   ____
6. Tenant agrees not to assign this Lease, nor to sublet any portion of the property, nor to allow any other person to live therein, without first obtaining written permission from Landlord. Further, it is agreed that covenants contained in this Lease, once breached, cannot afterward be performed, and that unlawful detainer proceedings may be commenced at once, without notice to Tenant.

7. Should any provision of this Lease be found to be invalid or unenforceable, the remainder of the Lease shall not be affected thereby and each term and provision herein shall be valid and enforceable to the fullest extent permitted by law.
8. All rights given to Landlord by this Lease shall be cumulative to any other laws which might exist or come into being. Any exercise or failure to exercise by Landlord of any right shall not act as a waiver of any other rights. No statement or promise of Landlord or his agent as to tenancy, repairs, alterations, or other terms and conditions shall be binding unless reduced to writing and signed by Landlord.
9. Tenant will be responsible for payment of all utilities, garbage, water and sewer charges, telephone, gas, association fees, or other bills incurred during the term of this Lease. Tenant specifically authorizes Landlord to deduct amounts of any unpaid bills from the Security deposit upon termination of this Agreement.
10. No rights of storage are given by this Agreement. Landlord shall not be liable for any loss of Tenant's property by fire, theft, breakage, burglary, or otherwise, nor for any accidental damage to persons or property in or about the leased premises resulting from electrical failure, water, rain, windstorm, etc., which may cause issue or flow into or from any part of said premises or improvements, including pipes, gas lines, sprinklers, or electrical connections, whether caused by the negligence of Landlord, Landlord's employees, contractors, agents, or by any other cause whatsoever. Tenant hereby agrees to make no claim for any such damages or loss against Landlord. **Tenant shall purchase renter's insurance.**
11. **IMPROVEMENTS TO PROPERTY** - Any improvements to the property made by Tenant inside or outside *must not be removed without written permission from the property manager*. This includes landscaping, scrubs, flowers, walkways, out buildings such as storage sheds and play-houses, etc. Any interior improvements the Tenant may have made to the property must also remain. Improvements such as but not limited to the following are installation of ceiling fans, book shelves, shelving, light fixtures, etc.
12. Any removal of Landlord's property without express written permission from the Landlord shall constitute abandonment and surrender of the premises and termination by the resident of this Agreement. Landlord may take immediate possession, exclude Tenant from property and store all Tenant's possessions at Tenant's expense pending reimbursement in full for Landlord's loss and damages.
13. Landlord has the right of emergency access to the leased premises at any time and access during reasonable hours to inspect the property or to show property to a prospective tenant or buyer. In the event that the property is sold, the lease/rental agreement between Landlord and Tenant is canceled on the date the new owner takes possession of property. Tenant has thirty days to vacate the property or sign new lease with new owner at new owner's option.
14. Tenant agrees to pay a Security Deposit of **$1,100.00** to bind Tenant's pledge of full compliance with the terms of this agreement. NOTE: SECURITY DEPOSIT MAY NOT BE USED TO PAY RENT! Any damages not previously reported as required in paragraph 25 will be repaired at Tenant's expense.
15. Release of the SECURITY DEPOSIT, at the Option of the Landlord is subject to the provisions below:
16. The full term of the Agreement has been completed.
17. No damage to the premises, buildings, or grounds is evident.

18. The entire dwelling, appliances, closets, and cupboards are to be clean and free from insects; the refrigerator is defrosted and clean; the range is to be clean including the racks and broiler pan; all windows are to be clean inside and outside; all debris and rubbish have been removed from the property; carpets have been commercially cleaned and left clean and odorless.
19. All unpaid charges have been paid including late charges, visitor charges, pet charges, delinquent rents, etc. WATER BILL MUST BE PAID IN FULL AND COPY OF PAID FINAL BILL SENT TO LANDLORD.
20. All keys have been returned.
21. A forwarding address for Tenant has been left with Landlord. Within thirty (30) days after termination of the occupancy, Landlord will mail the balance of the deposit to the address provided by Tenant in the names of all signatories hereto; or at the Option of Landlord will impose a claim on the deposit and so notify Tenant.
22. It is Tenant's responsibility to call, make arrangements, and be at residence to let meter readers in for final reading on gas, electric, and water. If Landlord has to do this, there is a $50 charge for each utility.
23. The acceptance by Landlord of partial payments of rent due shall not, under any circumstances, constitute a waiver of Landlord, nor affect any notice or legal proceeding in unlawful detainer theretofore given or commenced under state law. Acceptance of partial rent due or late payments does not create a custom nor constitute a continuing waiver of the obligation to pay on time. No payment by Tenant or receipt by Landlord of any amount of the monthly rent herein stipulated shall be deemed to be other than ***on account*** of the stipulated rent, nor shall any endorsement on any check or any letter accompanying such payment of rent be deemed an accord and satisfaction, but Landlord may accept such a partial payment without prejudice to his rights to collect the balance of such rent.
24. If Tenant leaves said premises unoccupied for fifteen (15) days while rent is due and unpaid, Landlord is granted the right hereunder to take immediate possession thereof and to exclude Tenant therefrom; removing all Tenant's property contained therein and placing it into storage at Tenant's expense.
25. Payment of rent may be made by check until the first check is returned unpaid. Regardless of cause, no additional payments may afterwards be made by check. Rent must then be made by cashier's check, money order or certified check.
26. Rent may be mailed through the United States Postal Service at Tenant's risk. Any rents lost in the mail will be treated as if unpaid until received by Landlord.
27. Tenant agrees, without protest, to reimburse Landlord for all actual and reasonable expenses incurred by way of Tenant's violation of any term or provision of this lease, including, but not limited to $10.00 for each Notice to Pay, Notice to Quit, or other notice mailed or delivered by Landlord to Tenant due to Tenant's non-payment of rent, all court costs and attorney's fees, and all costs of collection. Both Landlord and Tenant waive trial by jury and agree to submit to the personal jurisdiction and venue of a court of subject matter jurisdiction located in **Darrow** County, State of **Nita**. In such an event, no action shall be entertained by said court or any court of competent jurisdiction if filed more than one (1) year subsequent to the date the cause(s) of action accrued.
28. Tenant agrees to accept said dwelling and all of the furnishings and appliances therein as being in good and satisfactory condition unless a written statement of any objections is delivered to Landlord within three (3) days after resident takes possession. Tenant agrees

that failure to file such statement shall be conclusive proof that there were no defects in the property. Tenant agrees not to permit any damage to the premises during the period of this agreement to woodwork, floors, walls, furnishings, fixtures, appliances, windows, screens, doors, lawns, landscaping, fences, plumbing, electrical, air conditioning and heating, and mechanical systems. Tenant specifically agrees that he will be responsible for, and agrees to pay for, any damage done by rain, wind, or hail caused by leaving windows open; overflow of water or stoppage of waste pipes; breakage of glass; damage to screens; and deterioration of lawns and landscaping whether caused by drought, abuse, or neglect. Tenant agrees not to park or store a motor home, recreational vehicle, or trailer of any type on the premises.

29. Tenant's obligations are as follows:
30. Take affirmative action to insure that nothing is done which might place Landlord in violation of applicable building, housing, zoning, and health codes and regulations.
31. Keep the dwelling clean and sanitary, removing garbage and trash as it accumulates, and maintaining plumbing in good working order to prevent stoppages and leakage of plumbing fixtures, faucets, pipes, etc.
32. Operate all electrical, plumbing, sanitary, heating, ventilating, air conditioning, and other appliances in a reasonable, safe manner.
33. Assure that property belonging to Landlord is safeguarded against damage, destruction, loss, removal, or theft.
34. Conduct himself, his family, friends, guests, and visitors in a manner which will not disturb others.
35. Allow Landlord or Landlord's agent access to the premises for the purpose of inspection or repairs, or to show the property to someone else at reasonable hours, and to specifically authorize unannounced access anytime rent is late, or this Agreement is terminated or for pest control, maintenance estimates, serving legal notices, or emergencies. G. Comply with all provisions of this Agreement, particularly with respect to paying the rent on time and caring for the property. Tenant warrants that he will meet the above conditions in every respect, and acknowledges that failure to perform the obligations herein stipulated will be considered grounds for termination of this Agreement and loss of all deposits.
36. No additional locks will be installed on any door without written permission from Landlord. Landlord is to be provided duplicate keys for all locks so installed at Tenant's expense within twenty-four (24) hours of installation of said locks.
37. Tenant agrees to install and maintain a telephone, and to furnish Landlord the telephone number and/or any changes thereof within three (3) days of its installation.
38. In the event repairs are needed beyond the competence of Tenant, Tenant is urged to contact Landlord. Tenant is offered the discount as an incentive to make his own decisions on repairs to the property and to allow Landlord to rent the property without the need to employ professional management. Therefore, as much as possible, Tenant should refrain from contacting the Landlord or his agent except for emergencies, or for expensive repairs. Such involvement by the Landlord or his agent will result in the loss of the discount and/or deductible.
39. Tenant warrants that any work or repairs performed by him will be undertaken only if he is competent and qualified to perform them. Tenant will be totally responsible for all activities to ensure that work is done in a safe manner which will meet all the applicable codes and statutes. Tenant further warrants that he will be accountable for any mishaps and/or

accidents resulting from such work, and will hold Landlord free from harm, litigation, or claims of any other person.

40. Tenant is responsible for all plumbing repairs including faucets, leaks, stopped up pipes, frozen pipes, water damage, and bathroom caulking.
41. Appliances or furniture in the unit at date of lease per the attached "Exhibit A", are loaned, not leased, to Tenant. Maintenance of appliances or furniture is the responsibility of Tenant who will keep them in good repair.
42. Tenant is responsible for all glass, screen, and storm door repairs.
43. No money is to be deducted by Tenant from rent payment for any reason without express written permission of Landlord.
44. Regardless of assignment of responsibility, Tenant agrees to be responsible for the first $75.00 of any repair or maintenance required on the major systems of the property for the term of the lease. This deductible applies per occurrence.
45. Tenant accepts entirely the responsibility for the cleaning of furnaces or replacement of furnace filters.
46. Smoke detectors have been installed and are in operable condition in the following places: **Bedrooms and Kitchen**. From this time on Tenant will be required to maintain the smoke detectors. Any new batteries are Tenant's responsibility. If Tenant has any questions about the smoke detectors, they should call Landlord promptly.

    I/We, the undersigned, have personally checked the smoke alarms in the unit which is provided and find it/them to be in working order. I/We understand that the law requires me/us to maintain the alarm/s and keep fresh batteries in the mechanism. Tenant's failure to do so absolves Landlord, or agent from any responsibility for losses due to my/our non-compliance with the law or malfunction of the alarm.
47. NO WATER BEDS PERMITTED WITHOUT WRITTEN PERMISSION.
48. All parties agree that termination of this Agreement prior to termination date will constitute breach of the tenancy and all Security Deposits and one full month's rent shall be forfeited in favor of Landlord as liquidated damages, plus Tenant will be charged the cost of restoring the property to rental condition plus advertising and rent loss incurred until the new resident moves in. Tenant's liability for rent loss is limited to thirty (30) days after restoration is complete.
49. Properties built before and during the late sixties and early seventies may have had lead based products and asbestos products used in them. These products were considered to be safe at the time they were used, just as the building products used today are considered safe for home construction. Only the test of time will show which products are or are not safe to use. Having read the above, Tenant signs the lease below with the full understanding that these conditions may be present in this property. Tenant and all parties associated with this property relieve the owner, property manager, and any of his agents from any responsibilities for these conditions regardless of when or how these conditions were caused.

    Tenant also acknowledges receiving the EPA Booklet "Protect Your Family from Lead in Your Home"
50. In this Agreement the singular number where used will also include the plural, the masculine gender will also include the feminine; the term Landlord will include Owner or Lessor; and the term Tenant(s) will include Resident, Lessee, or Renter.

51. Tenant agrees to send all notices to Landlord or Property Manager in writing by certified mail, return receipt requested. This is the only form of notice permitted in a court hearing as evidence of notice given.

YOU SHOULD READ AND UNDERSTAND THIS LEASE, IT IS A LEGAL AND BINDING CONTRACT.

Signing below means you have read the Lease, are in full agreement with it, and have received a copy of the contract.

ACCEPTED THIS **28th** DAY OF **June, YR-1**.

Chris Montane — Tenant

Pat Hadden — Landlord

The following appliances and/or furniture are on loan to Tenant for the period of Tenant's rental agreement or lease on the following basis: Tenant agrees, by the signing of this agreement, that all appliances and/or furniture herein listed are accepted by Tenant, individually, as being in good working order or condition. Tenant agrees to maintain said appliances and/or furniture in good working order at his expense. If tenant fails to pay rent by the fifth (5th) day of the month, the landlord/manager or his representative may enter building and remove appliances or furniture belonging to Landlord without giving tenant advance notice.

APPLIANCES AND/OR FURNITURE

	Furniture Description	Appliance Number or Item	Condition	Location
1	**Refrigerator**		**Good**	**Kitchen**
2	**Stove**		**Fair**	**Kitchen**
3	**Microwave**		**Good**	**Kitchen**
4				
5				
6				
7				
8				
9				
10				
11				
12				
13				
14				
15				
16				

Tenant: *Chris Montane*

Date: *June 28, YR-1*

LANDLORD/TENANT COURT, COUNTY OF DARROW, STATE OF NITA

Case No. CR398

VERIFIED ANSWER FOR TERMINATION OF LEASE

CHRISTINE MONTANE

Plaintiff,

vs.

PAT HADDEN

Defendant.

The Defendant, Pat Hadden, by and through his attorney, Victoria Rogers, appearing, and as his answer to the Plaintiff's complaint, states:

1. Defendant, Pat Hadden, admits items 1 through 4 of the complaint and denies items 5 through 10 of the complaint.

2. Plaintiff is not entitled to termination of said lease for the following reasons:

a) The property located at 890 Front Street was free of any infestation of rats or vermin before Plaintiff occupied the residence. Plaintiff is therefore not in violation of a warranty of habitability under NRS 38-12-503 (1), (2) (a) & (b). In addition, Plaintiff failed to object that the property was not in good and satisfactory condition as set forth in the lease agreement at paragraph 21.

b) Defendant did not receive proper notice of any infestation of rats or vermin as specified in the lease or under NRS 38-12-503 (c) and is therefore not in violation of the warranty of habitability;

c) Plaintiff is a foreign national residing in the United States as a refugee and before resettlement in Nita City resided at the Houston Contract Detention Facility operated by U.S. Customs and Immigration and Customs Enforcement. Plaintiff's belongings were infested by bed bugs while she was resident at this facility. Any infestation of vermin was caused by Plaintiff. Defendant has not breached the warranty of habitability as described in NRS 38-12-503(3).

d) Plaintiff has regularly denied Defendant admittance into the residence at 890 Front Street, Nita City, Nita. Plaintiff's actions make it impossible for Defendant to resolve the problem. Plaintiff is in violation of paragraph 22 (F) of the lease that permits Landlord access to the premises for the purpose of inspection or repairs; or to show the property to someone else at reasonable hours; or to specifically authorize unannounced access anytime rent is late; or this Agreement is terminated; or for pest control, maintenance estimates, serving legal notices, or emergencies.

WHEREFORE, Defendant prays for judgment there is no breach of the lease for warranty of habitability, the lease continue, and Plaintiff take nothing by its Complaint.

CERTIFICATE OF MAILING

I certify that a true copy of the answer was mailed, postage prepaid, to:

Dated this 25th day of Month-2, YR-0.

Defendant's address:
Frazier & Dooley
239 Main Street, 4th Fl.
Nita City, Nita
555-423-6814

Victoria Rogers
Attorney for Pat Hadden

WITNESS STATEMENTS

Statement of Christine Montane

My name is Christine Montane. I live with my sister, Josephine, at 890 Front Street in Nita City. We rent our duplex from Pat Hadden. We moved into our house last year, in July.

My sister and I are living in the United States as refugees. The U.S. State Department granted us asylum from our mother country after our parents were assassinated by the leaders of the current government. This was about two years ago. I was a student at university, studying to become a nurse. My sister was still in high school. One night soldiers came to our home, broke down the door, and carried my father away. Three days later my mother went to the central prison to ask about my father. She never came home again. I never saw either of my parents again and I assume they have been killed. My sister and I took money my father had put aside for an emergency and we fled the country. Eventually, we ended up in Houston, Texas, where we asked for asylum. We were put in a detention camp in Houston until the U.S. government granted us refugee status. At that point we were relocated to Nita City with the help of Lutheran Family Services. We have resident status and hope to become U.S. citizens in five years. We know we can never go back to our homeland.

Lutheran Family Services helped us relocate to Nita City. They helped both my sister and I find employment, and assisted as we looked for housing. We used the last of our family money to get to Nita City, find a home, and buy furniture. Now we must live on any money we can make in our jobs. We also receive public assistance money to help us live. I received a scholarship to attend night school to finish my nursing studies. For now I work at Nita General Hospital as a nurse's aide. My sister has a part time job at the Yankee Doodle restaurant, where she works after school and on weekends. Our life is very different from when we lived in our homeland. It is difficult.

We first arrived in Nita City in June of last year. The person from Lutheran Family Services, Jan Sommerfeld, then worked with us to find a home and to find a job for me. She had a list of potential employers for me and I found a job right away. She helped us get on public assistance so we would have some money for food and necessities, especially because my new wages would barely cover the costs of rent and food. She also had a list of places we could rent to live. She drove us around for an afternoon to show us possible locations. My sister and I were not sure about many of the places that were available. We did not think the neighborhoods looked safe for two young single women. The price of rent was also so high that we did not have many choices. The best choice seemed to be the duplex house owned by Mr. Hadden on Front Street.

The house on Front Street was in a neighborhood that was not far from my new job or my sister's school. We could both walk or take the bus. The house was neat and tidy when we visited. Of course we did not inspect the place with magnifying glasses so we had no idea it was infested with those terrible bugs. Jan Sommerfeld helped us with the lease and we moved in on July 1, YR-1.

We had to purchase some new furniture and Lutheran Family Services gave us some nice things that had been donated. We bought new beds and dressers for each of us from the money we got from our father. We received a nice couch, a chair, and a table and chairs for eating and doing homework. Finally, about the middle of July we settled in for our new life in America. It was all like one big happy dream after all the terrible things that had happened to us.

Almost immediately we found out that living in America was not what we had envisioned. The first thing that happened was a workman came into the house unannounced. My sister was in the shower and when she got out she found this man standing there staring at her. My sister screamed and the man told her he was there to fix the toilet. She told him to leave immediately. When I came home that evening she told me what had happened. I was so angry. I immediately tried to call Mr. Hadden to complain. He did not answer his phone. Then I wrote him a letter and told him that unless they were announced in advance we would no longer allow workmen into the house.

The people living in the other half of the duplex were not the best neighbors. Shortly after we moved in the disturbances began. Our neighbors were a couple who always seemed to be fighting or making a lot of noise. When we first moved in my sister prepared a traditional dish for them as a way of making friends. When she delivered the dish she saw the house was very messy and dirty. The woman was not especially nice and my sister said she appeared to be intoxicated. A couple of times the police came to their house because of the fighting. One of our other neighbors told me it was domestic abuse and the man had been arrested and taken away. Not long after that they moved out.

Then Mr. Hadden, the landlord, had a whole bunch of people come and clean out the place next door. It took them several days to clear out the things and garbage. Some workmen came to paint and they did other things that made our house smell badly for a few days. Maybe it was paint but I think it smelled of insecticide.

My sister started attending school in August of YR-1. She was enrolled in the 11th grade at the local high school. Because we did not have much money she also found a job. She was working after school and on weekends at a local restaurant, The Yankee Doodle. It is a very nice place where they serve good, wholesome, American food. My sister tells me it is "fast food" and we laugh when we imagine seeing the food running around the kitchen.

In September YR-1 my sister started to complain that she had a rash on her legs and back. She had these red bumps that were itching her. At first we thought it was simply because we were not adjusted to the cold winter weather and how dry it was in our house. I asked some people at the hospital where I work about what to do for the rash. They suggested some simple remedies such as lotions or bathing in baking soda. My sister tried those things but they did not help her.

Then I started getting the rash as well. It was most noticeable in the mornings after I got out of bed. The lotions helped to sooth the itch but did not help it go away. I was getting worried about the condition and asked one of the nurses at the hospital where I work about it. She told me it looked like bites and that we should see a doctor.

At the same time my sister started to get teased at school. Her legs had all these red bumps on them and her classmates made fun of her. The people at work also started to comment about the marks on her legs and arms. My sister was very upset that she could not make friends and that people were laughing at her.

We finally went to the clinic at my hospital. The nice doctor took one look at our rashes and told us it was not a rash but bites! Bites from bed bugs. My sister and I were mortified by this news. Bed bugs suggest we are not clean and that our house is not clean. This could not be true—but it was. The doctor gave us some ointment to help with the bites and a pamphlet that told us what to do to get rid of these creatures.

I did not know what to do. I was so embarrassed. I had no idea how we had been infested by bed bugs. When we went home I checked our beds and sure enough there were signs of bed bugs on the mattresses. I went to the store where we purchased the beds and the salesmen assured me the beds were brand new and could not have been the source. He reminded me the beds came wrapped in plastic from the factory. I'm sure he was correct. I called Jan Sommerfeld at Lutheran Family Services to ask about the furniture they had given to us. Jan Sommerfeld assured me that they completely check any items donated before they provide them to families. She let me know that if they ever find signs of insects they immediately destroy the item and it is never provided to someone in need. I told her that before we came to Nita City we did not have bed bugs. She suggested the bugs had already been in our duplex and said I should contact the landlord. He was responsible.

I tried to call Pat Hadden, the landlord, several times. He never returned my telephone calls. After about five days of trying to reach him I sent him a letter telling him about the bed bugs. He did not really respond. I then sent him an email and he finally called me. He was not very nice. He told me that he had never had any problems with bed bugs before we moved into the duplex. He told me it was our responsibility to take care of the pests. Then he said he would send someone over to see about the problem and hung up.

A few days later that horrible man came to the house. My sister told him to go away when he came to the door. Later she said he told her he was there to see about the problem with bed bugs but that she said he could not come in. Mr. Hadden did not follow the instructions in my letter about calling first so we felt it was OK to send that Peeping Tom away, even if he was there about the bugs.

The next day Jan Sommerfeld called with some suggestions. She told us to wash all of our linens and place them in a hot dryer for twenty minutes. We had to put our other things in plastic bags. Then we were to locate the bugs hiding places. They hide in places like your alarm clock, your picture frames, inside your mattress, electrical outlets, under baseboards, and inside any wall cracks. We then had to vacuum all these areas and treat them with heat and then apply a pesticide dust. After applying the pesticide we had to seal everything up, from the cracks in the walls to tears in the box spring to adding covers that completely seal the mattress. This took a great deal of time and all of our extra money.

Sadly, our efforts did not work. Within a month we were getting bug bites again. I called Jan Sommerfeld and told her that our efforts had failed. She finally suggested that I find a lawyer to try and help us. She gave me the number of the Legal Services Office in Nita City. The next day I called and they set an appointment for me. I spoke with a very nice lawyer who told me Mr. Hadden was not following the law. He told me the best thing to do was to try to get out of our lease and that he would help us with our problem. Even if we do get out of the lease and find a better place to live we are in a bad way. I'm sure the bugs are living in our mattresses and furniture. We cannot get the bugs out and must dispose of them. We have no money for new furniture and had no insurance on our household belongings. I am also afraid that rent at a new place will be more money than we are paying at the duplex.

I admit my sister is having a hard time adjusting to our new life. She misses our parents and does not like her new school. She is not making good friends. She admitted to me that the reason she was home on the day Mr. Santini came to the house is because she had been sent home from school for bad behavior. I found out that she had been skipping classes to go out with others from her school. This is not usually like my sister and I have had stern words with her about these bad behaviors. She is now back in school and doing better.

I do admit that while we were living at the duplex on Front Street that we invited other refugees from our homeland to stay with us while they found a place to live. Usually people would stay for from two to five days before leaving. Our guests started to stay with us beginning in August YR-1. Sometimes we would have others from our country over to the house to celebrate our freedom from the repressive regime in our homeland. These celebrations were never unruly or caused trouble. No one, including Mr. Hadden, ever spoke to me about this matter and I do not understand why he is now saying that we were bad tenants and trouble makers.

Signed,

Christine Montane

Christine Montane
29th day of Month-1

Statement of Jan Sommerfeld

My name is Jan Sommerfeld. I work for Lutheran Family Services (LFS) here in Nita City. Lutheran Family Services Nita is a faith based, non-profit human service agency helping children and families during their most challenging times. We have been committed to serving all people, regardless of race, religion, sex, or age since 1948. I specifically work in the Refugee and Asylee Program at LFS. The Lutheran Family Services (LFS) Refugee & Asylee Programs are dedicated to helping refugees, asylum seekers, and internally displaced persons and their families rebuild their lives by equipping them to achieve self-sufficiency within their first year in the United States, and fostering integration into their new communities.

I have an undergraduate degree in international studies from the University of Nita and my masters in social work from the University of Denver. I personally have been helping people who are living with a very uncertain future for about twenty years.

I first met Christine Montane in June, YR-1. Ms. Montane and her sister, Josephine, were being moved to Nita City from a contract detention facility in Houston, Texas. The Montanes had been housed in this facility until they received asylum status under the United States Refugee Program (USRP). I believe they had been living in the facility for several months before being admitted to the United States. LFS helped the Montane sisters receive their status and agreed to help them in their relocation by giving them a sponsor assurance.

The Montane sisters' story is one that is all too common. Their parents had both been taken and killed by a hostile regime in Africa. They had been fortunate to escape their country with some family money and flee to the United States. A refugee is defined as a person outside of his or her country of nationality who is unable or unwilling to return because of persecution or a well-founded fear of persecution on account of race, religion, nationality, membership in a particular social group, or political opinion.

LFS arranged transportation from Houston to Nita City. I met them at the bus station and brought them to our offices. We spent the next several hours discussing their immediate needs and talking about possibilities. I then got them settled with a host family where they stayed until we found them full time housing. The next day I took Christine to Nita General Hospital where she was able to find a job as a nurse's aide. We then picked up her sister and went to see some rental units and apartments. We looked at several and they decided on a duplex at 890 Front Street in Nita City. LSC has previously worked with the landlord, Pat Hadden, and never had any problems with him or his properties.

After finding them a new home I helped the Montanes open a bank account and find some furniture for their duplex. They purchased new beds and bedding. LFS gave them furniture that was donated by parishioners in Nita City. LFS' policy for accepting donations is the furniture must be in good condition. We have workers at our collection center check all donations to ensure they are in good condition and do not have any problems such as bed bugs. We got the Montane sisters moved in and settled during the first week of July, YR-1. I helped them both enroll for classes, Christine in evening classes to finish her nursing degree and Josephine in public high school. I also helped Josephine find a part time job at a fast food restaurant. The last thing I did was help then get public assistance in the form of food stamps and medical care. At that point my initial work with them was completed. My job responsibilities were then to check in on them periodically to make sure they were adjusting to life in the United States, to make suggestions about attending social functions offered by LFS and local Lutheran churches, and to work with them on ensuring they were able to complete the programs to make them eligible for status as lawful permanent residents and then, after five years, naturalized citizens. I believed the Montane sisters are perfect candidates for citizenship and would be successful in adapting to life in the United States.

I had limited contact with the Montane sisters until September YR-1 when Christine Montane contacted me to tell me of a problem she was having with bed bugs. She first wanted to know if the furniture LFS had provided could have been infested. I assured her that nothing provided by LFS would have contained bed bugs or eggs. She told me both she and her sister were covered with bites and were so ashamed that people would think them unclean. I assured her that bed bugs had become a serious problem in the United States and there was no longer a stigma associated with a bed bug infestation. I suggested she contact her landlord to report the problem and ask for his assistance. She let me know she had already left a telephone message for Pat Hadden but had not received a reply.

Two days later I contacted Ms. Montane to offer her some suggestions on how to get rid of the bed bugs. She let me know she had not had a return call from her landlord. I let her know that the remedies I suggested were highly recommend and should help her with her problem. The next week I again called to check on the problem. Ms. Montane told me she had done all of the things I suggested and the problem seemed to have gone away. I was relieved but told her to keep in touch. About one month later I heard again from Ms. Montane. She said that her bed bug problem had returned and that she was not able to get any help from her landlord. At this point I called Nita Legal Services and asked for their advice. They suggested I put Ms. Montane in contact with them and they would try to break her lease for a violation of warranty of habitability. I wasn't sure what that meant but called Ms. Montane and encouraged her to get help from a lawyer. I gave her the contact information for Nita Legal Services.

I also tried to speak with Pat Hadden about this problem. In the past Mr. Hadden had been a helpful resource for our organization and provided housing for reasonable prices to those we were assisting. This time Mr. Hadden failed to return my call. Based upon what has occurred with this situation I do not think LFS will work with Mr. Hadden in the future. The people we work with have been traumatized. They have no need for poor treatment now that they are in a safe haven. It only reinforces the negative things that have happened in their lives. If Nita Legal Services is able to get the Montane sisters out of their lease we will make sure they get proper housing for the future. I also feel quite badly about them having to get rid of their furniture and we will do what we can to help them find new beds.

I do not know anything about the Montane sisters having wild parties at their house. I do know they have tried to work within their own refugee community to welcome new refugees to Nita City. I believe they miss their homeland greatly and anything they can do to help ease their pain of relocation and their own personal losses is a good thing for them psychologically and emotionally.

Signed,

Jan Sommerfeld

Jan Sommerfeld
3rd day of Month-1

Statement of Pat Hadden

My name is Pat Hadden. I own a number of residential rental properties in Nita City, including the duplex at 890/892 Front Street, Nita City. In addition to owning rental properties I work full time as a sales agent for Acurrato Medical Products, an innovative medical device company that produces medical devices for the post-acute healthcare market. I probably spend eighty percent of my time with my sales job for Acurrato and twenty percent of my time managing my rental properties.

Most of my properties are either single family homes or duplexes. All but one of the six properties are in Nita City proper with one located in the adjacent suburbs. Except for the suburban unit I would say all of the units are for the lower income tenant. Just the same I want to take good care of my tenants. I always make sure my rental properties are in good shape for the people who live in them. Before the Montane sisters moved into my duplex on Front Street I never had a problem with a tenant complaining about the unit. I certainly never had a problem with bed bugs.

Whenever a tenant vacates one of my units I inspect it to make sure they have left it in good shape. If the unit needs to be painted I have a crew come in and put on a fresh coat of paint in all rooms. If a unit has not been painted in six years I have it painted whether it is in need or not. If it is needed I have a cleaning crew go through the house and make sure the kitchen and bathrooms are in good shape. We require when a tenant moves out they have the carpets cleaned. If they do not take care of the cleaning we have a carpet cleaning company come and do all of the carpets in the unit.

I admit that when I replace appliances I use lower quality or lightly used fixtures. After all, these units are not luxury units. The rent prices for my units are always on the median for comparable units. I charge a fair price so I can pay my own expenses and mortgages.

I have worked with Lutheran Family Services for a number of years. I appreciate the plight of many of the people they serve and do my best to provide a healthy new environment as these people readjust and become functioning members of society. The people they recommend usually only stay for one or two years. Once they are established and making a fair living they usually move to more expensive housing. I'm proud of my role in taking care of people who have to flee their homes. This is the first time I've had a bad experience with someone who has refugee status.

In late June of YR-1 I received a call from Jan Sommerfeld of Lutheran Family Services. I've worked with Jan off and on for a number of years. She sometimes calls to see if I have a unit available for a refugee family. Until now I always tried to accommodate Jan. On this occasion she asked if I had something available for two refugee sisters from a country in Africa. She told me their parents had been murdered and they had just arrived from Texas with refugee status.

As it happened I had half of my duplex at 890/892 Front Street available at that time. We had just finished cleaning the unit and having it repainted when I received the call from Jan. I offered to show them the unit the next day. I met Sommerfeld, Christine Montane, and Josephine Montane at the unit. They liked what they saw and I had them complete the lease information and sign the lease. I gave them the keys and went back to my other job. The Montane's moved into the unit shortly thereafter.

About the middle of July I received a message from Christine Montane saying the sink in the bathroom would not stop running. I sent a work order to Joe Santini to do the repair. Joe Santini is a private contractor who does all my repair and remodeling work. My company is really too small to have a staff so I contract out things like repairs and cleaning to people I trust. I've worked with Joe pretty much since I started investing in rental properties. He always does a great job in a timely fashion - something that keeps my tenants happy. I've never had a complaint about Joe or any of his crew since I've been using them. You can imagine my surprise when I got this angry telephone message and then the letter from Christine Montane saying one of my workers was in the house leering at her naked sister. I immediately called Joe Santini and asked him what had happened. He told me that he had gone to the duplex to fix the sink. When he rang the bell no one answered so he let himself into the unit and went to the bathroom to make the repair. Joe told me that almost as soon as he got to the door a young woman got out of the shower, looked at him and started screaming. He claims he muttered an apology and left immediately. Joe is not the kind of guy who would do what the Montane sister's claim. I tried to call Christine Montane to apologize but she does not have an answering system for her phone. I guess since I could not reach her I let the matter pass.

I did have some trouble with the tenants living in the other half of the duplex, 892 Front Street, when the Montane sisters first moved into their unit. I evicted them because of several reported instances of domestic violence. Those types of situations are never good for a rental. They disturb the neighbors, cause the police to intervene, usually tear up the unit, and, of course, cause harm to the person being abused. After I received notice of the third reported instance of domestic violence I evicted those tenants under the terms of the lease. Needless to say they did not leave the place in very good shape. There was damage to the walls, and they broke light fixtures and the kitchen faucet. In addition, the place was a mess. I had to hire Mr. Santini to do extensive work to repair and repaint the whole unit. The tenants left some of their furniture and I had to have it hauled away. I also had to hiring a cleaning crew to come and clean out the kitchen and bathroom. They also had to clean the carpet in all of the rooms. Finally, Joe Santini had to do work to get rid of roaches in the kitchen. If the Montane sisters smelled pesticide it must be from when they treated for roaches. There were no reports of bed bugs from Santini, the cleaning crew, or the exterminator. I'm confident there were no bed bugs in the 892 Front Street unit.

Bed bugs are a bad business and once you have them it is really difficult to get rid of them. I try to follow both the rental housing and hotel market in Nita to track things such as rental trends and other matters. I know bed bugs are a big problem on the national scene but so far they are not largely reported in Nita City. I am confident there was no bed bug infestation in my duplex before the Montane sisters moved into the unit. I know the Montane sisters are claiming the bed bugs were either in their unit when they moved in or came from next door. I'm sure this is not the case. I would have had reports from previous tenants or my crews if this was the situation.

I'm now faced with the situation that my unit does have bed bugs. It's going to cost a great deal to get rid of these pests now that they are in the unit. It will cost several thousand dollars to replace all the carpets and drapes, fumigate all the rooms, fill existing cracks, and monitor for the next year. In addition, I now have to let future tenants know about the problem. You know that will have a chilling effect on my ability to rent the units.

I did try to respond to Christine Montane's complaints about the bed bugs when she first reported them to me. She claims I did not respond to her calls. I did call her back but she never answers her phone and there is no message machine. She also made it impossible for me to respond with any assistance because she refuses to let any repair people into the unit without her being present. When I sent Joe Santini to deal with the problem they refused to let him in. She and her sister are only there in the evenings and I can't get a crew to work in the evenings. She would not even respond to calls from the exterminator I tried to hire to fumigate the unit. These women are trying to paint me as the bad guy when they are the ones who caused the problem. I really have done my best to help them out but they put up roadblocks.

I am really sure that my duplex was not infested with bed bugs before the Montane sisters took possession. I think they must have brought the bugs with them when they moved in. They may not have recognized they were the carriers but there could be no other way it happened. When I got served with the papers for this law suit I did some investigating on my own. I found information online that the facility where the Montane sisters were housed before they came to Nita City had a bed bug infestation while they were there. It was reported on the local news channel and I got copies of the story. Bed bugs spread by hitch hiking in luggage and on clothing. I can't prove the bugs specifically were introduced into my duplex by the Montane sisters but this situation is as likely a source as the bugs already being present when they moved in.

I also know the Montane sisters had frequent overnight guests staying with them. I understand that these "guests" would be people from their homeland who were also refugees. They would arrive, stay for two or three days, and then go somewhere else. Initially I had some concern that the Montane sisters were violating their lease by letting others live with them. Through a neighbor I learned the people never stayed more than a few days at any one time. The story the sisters told the neighbor was their guests had also escaped from their homeland and were trying to make a new life in American. The Montanes were letting them stay until they found permanent lodging of their own. I decided to let this slide as I did not want to appear heartless when it came to refugees. I guess this was a big mistake because if the Montanes did not bring the bed bugs with them they came in through these "guests."

I know it might be easier to let the Montanes out of their lease but this is a matter of principle at this point. I am not at fault for the bed bug problem and it will now be difficult to rent the unit after I disclose the problem. I think it is fair that since they brought the bugs with them they have to stay for the term of the lease. If things were really fair they should have to pay to have the pests eradicated from my property.

Signed,

Pat Hadden

Pat Hadden
3rd day of Month-1

Statement of Joseph Santini

My name is Joseph H. Santini, but everyone calls me Joe. I have my own handyman business here in Nita City. I've been working all my life in the construction trade. My father was in the business before me and my younger brother Arnold is a building super here in Nita City. You can say my whole family knows about construction and home repair. Most of my business is either in home or business remodeling or contract maintenance. I have a standing contract with Pat Hadden to do all of the repairs and remodeling for the rental units he owns. I've been doing this for Pat since he started his business.

Most of the work I do for Pat is simple repairs. Things like fixing a busted sink or replacing a hot water heater. Sometimes I have to do more extensive things like painting, fixing holes in dry wall, replacing broken windows, installing new appliances and fixtures, and other stuff like that. Mostly I do the work but I also have a couple of guys that work for me when a project is bigger. One time we had to gut a house for Pat and redo the whole interior. Pat and I work well together and we trust each other. Mostly we do business with a handshake.

Pat's duplex on Front Street has sure been a big headache for him this past year. It also didn't make my life any easier either. Sure it means some money in my pocket for the repairs and getting rid of the roaches, and now the bed bugs, but it has created a lot of heartache for both of us.

My heartache came from the accusation by that young women living in 890 Front Street. She accused me of being some kind of pervert and that just isn't right. It was all an innocent mistake. This was in July of YR-1. I got a report that the sink was not working in that unit. I stopped by to fix the problem and got myself into a world of trouble. Like I always do, I rang the doorbell and knocked on the door. When no one answered the door I let myself into the unit and went to the bathroom. Just as I'm in the doorway I hear the shower running and then a naked girl gets out of the shower. I was stunned and just stood there for a second. She takes a look at me and starts screaming like I was raping her or something. I stammered an apology and backed out. Then I got a call from Pat about me standing there and leering at the girl while she was naked. If I was there for thirty seconds I would be surprised. Just the same, my credibility with Pat is now not so hot. When I have to go back to 890 Front Street I need to call first and make an appointment. It's a pain in the rear. I'm almost sixty years old. I certainly do not get my jollies from peeping at girls where I fix sinks. The last time I was at 890 I tried to call but got no answer. I went to the door and saw one of the girls inside. She refused to let me in. I told Pat and he said he would hire someone else to do the work.

The other half of the duplex, 892 Front Street, was where I also did work for Pat in August YR-1. Pat evicted the people living there and they left the place in a shambles. These folks really had some anger management issues or something. The place was torn up and we had to do a lot of work on the place. We had to replace some of the cabinets in the kitchen, get rid of the appliances, paint the whole unit, replace some of the carpet and clean the rest, and fix some light fixtures. The kitchen was infested with roaches and we had to do a lot of work trying to make sure we got rid of them. The only bugs we found in 892 were roaches. There were no signs of bed bugs and all the work we did in getting rid of the roaches would certainly have taken care of any other pests as well.

Getting rid of roaches is a bit like going to war - you got to have a plan to succeed. Before you start spraying pesticides on every open surface in an attempt to kill the roaches, you need to strategize. Plotting out an attack on a group of insects may sound borderline crazy, but you'll have more success if you plan ahead.

Roaches need three things to make them happy - warm shelter, something to eat, and water. If you want to evict these critters you take away those things. Using a pesticide will not permanently do the job.

First, you need to figure out where the bugs have set up camp. I set up traps to find where they live. While I'm waiting for results I make sure to clean up potential places that serve as feeding troughs. This includes things like piles of papers, boxes, or bags. Actually, any piles of clutter make for happy meals for roaches. These guys are drawn to paper products because they leave their smell on them. It's like a G.P.S. system for bugs. It communicates the insects' locations to other ones around and leaves a trail for them to find their ways back and forth.

The second thing we do is to either seriously clean the appliances or replace them. This includes the stove, microwave, and the refrigerator. You have to get up every spot of grease and dirt on and around them. You really have to get rid of any grease because even small spots of it are like foie gras for roaches.

Next you have to eliminate their watering holes. We check for all sources of standing water, including the drip pan under the refrigerator, condensation around pipes, and the sink. We want to make sure the place is dry—no faucets dripping, covering the drains, etc.

The last thing we do is fill any cracks where the roaches could live. We caulk them closed to seal them out of the living space. We also use boric acid dust as that stuff kills them dead. Before we caulk we add some dust. Anything we can't seal we also cover with the powder. This includes under the sink, behind the appliances, and on top of the cabinets. I try not to use pesticides if possible. They usually do not work as well as the process I just described and you have to follow EPA regulations. If you follow those steps it usually takes care of any bugs you have. When you're up against insects that outlasted dinosaurs it takes a multi-tiered battle plan. Yes, it would also have had the same effect on bed bugs. However, we never saw any signs of bed bugs when we were working on 892 Front Street.

I do believe that Pat took the extra step of having an exterminator apply pesticide as well. I told him he didn't need it with the steps we took but he wanted to be extra careful. Roaches can be a serious problem.

I do not believe that by sealing the cracks in 892 Front Street we diverted any insects to the unit sharing the common wall. By dusting before we sealed the cracks it would have poisoned any bugs in the area. This was a thorough job, done by the book. I'll stand by my work.

Most of the units owned by Pat Hadden are for lower income families. Just the same, he takes good care of his real estate and tenants. I would not call him a slum lord but a savvy property owner who does his best to maintain his investments.

I do not believe that the things I am saying will have any effect on Pat's decision to hire me for future work.

Signed,

Joseph Santini

Joseph Santini
5th day of Month-1

SWORN STATEMENT OF VIRGINIA HOECKLE

My name is Virginia Hoeckle. I have lived at 971 Front Street in Nita City for the past sixty-five years. I'm now eighty-six years old. I've been a widow for the past fifteen years. My children live away from Nita City so I only see them occasionally.

Since I've lived in the neighborhood for so many years I know just about everyone who lives on the 800 block of Front Street. Things have changed over the years as first families lived in the area and then, as Nita City grew, families moved to the suburbs. We decided to stay on Front Street. My husband, Ralph, was a bus driver and I never worked. He always said my job was to make sure the kids were raised properly.

Well, the neighborhood is not anything like what it was when we first bought our house. My husband had just left the service and we used his benefits to buy our little house. When we first moved in everyone on the street was alike - lots of nice families with the same values. Now it's a real melting pot. We have single people, married people, and couples living together. People of lots of different color - it's a regular United Nations on Front Street with people from Asia, Mexico, and even Africa all living on the street. My husband would have liked it now. He once told me our neighborhood was too "white bread." I remember we laughed about it.

I do know just about everybody on the street. It's kind of hard for me to get around these days. The nice people next door have their children get my groceries for me - a real nice couple. Most of the time I either sit on my front porch or in the living room where I can get a good look at what is going on. I like it when I can sit outside because I can chat with my neighbors as they go past.

I do know the Montane sisters, especially Josephine who is the younger of the two. Josie will stop and talk to me when she comes home from school or when she is done with her work. She is a hard working girl. It's a terrible thing that happened to her parents. I can't imagine having to leave my home in the middle of the night because someone was coming to kill me. They are certainly brave girls. I hear they may be moving out because of bugs. That's a bad thing. I hope they didn't bring them when they moved in. I don't know what I would do if I got bugs.

The Montanes do have lots of people who come to visit. Sometimes it's like Grand Central Station with whole families staying with them for days. Josie tells me these are people from her homeland who have also fled from the tyranny. These folks show up toting all manner of possessions and suitcases. They stay for a couple of days and then they are gone. I don't know how they can sometime crowd all those people into that little house.

I know the man who owns that duplex, Mr. Hadden. He's also a nice fellow. When he bought the place it was in pretty bad shape. He fixed it up and takes care to see that the people who live there take care of the yard. Mr. Hadden sometimes comes to visit with me to talk about the people who live there. Once I complained about folks who were having these wild parties in his house. Next thing I knew they had moved out and nice new folks were living there. He did come by and talk to me about the Montane sisters. He asked me a whole bunch of questions about the people who would come and visit. I let him know it was no big deal and it was a good thing the girls were doing by helping these people on their way to a new life.

I'm sorry those sisters and Mr. Hadden are not getting along. I don't know whose fault it is about the bugs but I do hope they do something about them.

Signed,

Virginia Hoeckle

Virginia Hoeckle
10th day of Month-1

Mrs. Hoeckle made this statement under oath. Opposing counsel had the opportunity to ask questions during the deposition. She is not available for trial. However, neither counsel knew at the time of the deposition that she would be unable to provide live testimony.

Selected Statutory Materials from Nita Revised Statutes

NRS §38-12-507. Breach of warranty of habitability - tenant's remedies.

(1) If there is a breach of the warranty of habitability as set forth in section 38-12-503 (2), the following provisions shall apply:

(a) Upon no less than ten and no more than thirty days written notice to the landlord specifying the condition alleged to breach the warranty of habitability and giving the landlord five business days from the receipt of the written notice to remedy the breach, a tenant may terminate the rental agreement by surrendering possession of the dwelling unit. If the breach is remediable by repairs, the payment of damages, or otherwise and the landlord adequately remedies the breach within five business days of receipt of the notice, the rental agreement shall not terminate by reason of the breach.

(b) A tenant may obtain injunctive relief for breach of the warranty of habitability in any court of competent jurisdiction. In any proceeding for injunctive relief, the court shall determine actual damages for a breach of the warranty at the time the court orders the injunctive relief. A landlord shall not be subject to any court order for injunctive relief if the landlord tenders the actual damages to the court within two business days of the order. Upon application by the tenant, the court shall immediately release to the tenant the damages paid by the landlord. If the tenant vacates the leased premises, the landlord shall not be permitted to rent the premises again until such time as the unit would be in compliance with the warranty of habitability set forth in section 38-12-503 (1).

(c) In an action for possession based upon nonpayment of rent in which the tenant asserts a defense to possession based upon the landlord's alleged breach of the warranty of habitability, upon the filing of the tenant's answer the court shall order the tenant to pay into the registry of the court all or part of the rent accrued after due consideration of expenses already incurred by the tenant based upon the landlord's breach of the warranty of habitability.

NRS §38-12-503. Warranty of habitability.

(1) In every rental agreement, the landlord is deemed to warrant that the residential premises is fit for human habitation.

(2) A landlord breaches the warranty of habitability set forth in subsection (1) of this section if:

(a) A residential premises is uninhabitable as described in section 38-12-505 or otherwise unfit for human habitation; and

(b) The residential premises is in a condition that is materially dangerous or hazardous to the tenant's life, health, or safety; and

(c) The landlord has received written notice of the condition described in paragraphs (a) and (b) of this subsection (2) and failed to cure the problem within a reasonable time.

(3) When any condition described in subsection (2) of this section is caused by the misconduct of the tenant, a member of the tenant's household, a guest or invitee of the tenant, or a person under the tenant's direction or control, the condition shall not constitute a breach of the warranty of habitability. It shall not be misconduct by a victim of domestic violence or domestic abuse under this subsection (3) if the condition is the result of domestic violence or domestic abuse and the landlord has been given written notice and evidence of domestic violence or domestic abuse as described in section 38-12-402 (2) (a).

(4) In response to the notice sent pursuant to paragraph (c) of subsection (2) of this section, a landlord may, in the landlord's discretion, move a tenant to a comparable unit after paying the reasonable costs, actually incurred, incident to the move.

(5) Except as set forth in this part 5, any agreement waiving or modifying the warranty of habitability shall be void as contrary to public policy.

(6) Nothing in this part 5 shall:

(a) Prevent a landlord from terminating a rental agreement as a result of a casualty or catastrophe to the dwelling unit without further liability to the landlord or tenant; or

(b) Preclude a landlord from initiating an action for nonpayment of rent, breach of the rental agreement, violation of section 38-12-504, or as provided for under article 40 of title 13, NRS.

NRS §38-12-505. Uninhabitable residential premises.

(1) A residential premises is deemed uninhabitable if it substantially lacks any of the following characteristics:

(a) Waterproofing and weather protection of roof and exterior walls maintained in good working order, including unbroken windows and doors;

(b) Plumbing or gas facilities that conformed to applicable law in effect at the time of installation and that are maintained in good working order;

(c) Running water and reasonable amounts of hot water at all times furnished to appropriate fixtures and connected to a sewage disposal system approved under applicable law;

(d) Functioning heating facilities that conformed to applicable law at the time of installation and that are maintained in good working order;

(e) Electrical lighting, with wiring and electrical equipment that conformed to applicable law at the time of installation, maintained in good working order;

(f) Common areas and areas under the control of the landlord that are kept reasonably clean, sanitary, and free from all accumulations of debris, filth, rubbish, and garbage and that have appropriate extermination in response to the infestation of rodents or vermin;

(g) Appropriate extermination in response to the infestation of rodents or vermin throughout a residential premises;

(h) An adequate number of appropriate exterior receptacles for garbage and rubbish, in good repair;

(i) Floors, stairways, and railings maintained in good repair;

(j) Locks on all exterior doors and locks or security devices on windows designed to be opened that are maintained in good working order; or

(k) Compliance with all applicable building, housing, and health codes, which, if violated, would constitute a condition that is dangerous or hazardous to a tenant's life, health, or safety.

(2) No deficiency in the common area shall render a residential premises uninhabitable as set forth in subsection (1) of this section, unless it materially and substantially limits the tenant's use of his or her dwelling unit.

(3) Unless otherwise stated in section 38-12-506, prior to being leased to a tenant, a residential premises must comply with the requirements set forth in section 38-12-503 (1), (2) (a), and (2)(b).

Exhibits

Exhibit 1

Christine Montane
890 Front Street
Nita City, Nita

Dear Mr. Hadden,

We have discovered bed bugs living in our house. My sister has bites all over her legs and arms and is quite uncomfortable. I write to inform you about this problem and request you provide a service to get rid of these horrible creatures.

When we moved to your duplex we had just arrived in Nita City from the relocation camp in Houston, Texas. We purchased beds and other furniture so I know we did not bring the bugs with us when we moved into the house. I can only imagine the bugs were already in the house when we moved in or they have come from the people who live in the unit next door.

No matter where they have come from they must go. Please have someone take care of this problem right away. I fear we will have to dispose of our beds, furniture, and clothing as a result.

As I told you before, we no longer feel comfortable when you have workmen come to our house unannounced. The last experience was quite unpleasant for my sister and we want to avoid the same situation. Please contact me in advance of when we should expect someone to rid us of these creatures.

Sincerely,

Chris Montane

Exhibit 2

EMAIL SENT TO PAT HADDEN BY CHRISTINE MONTANE – 5TH DAY OF MONTH-4

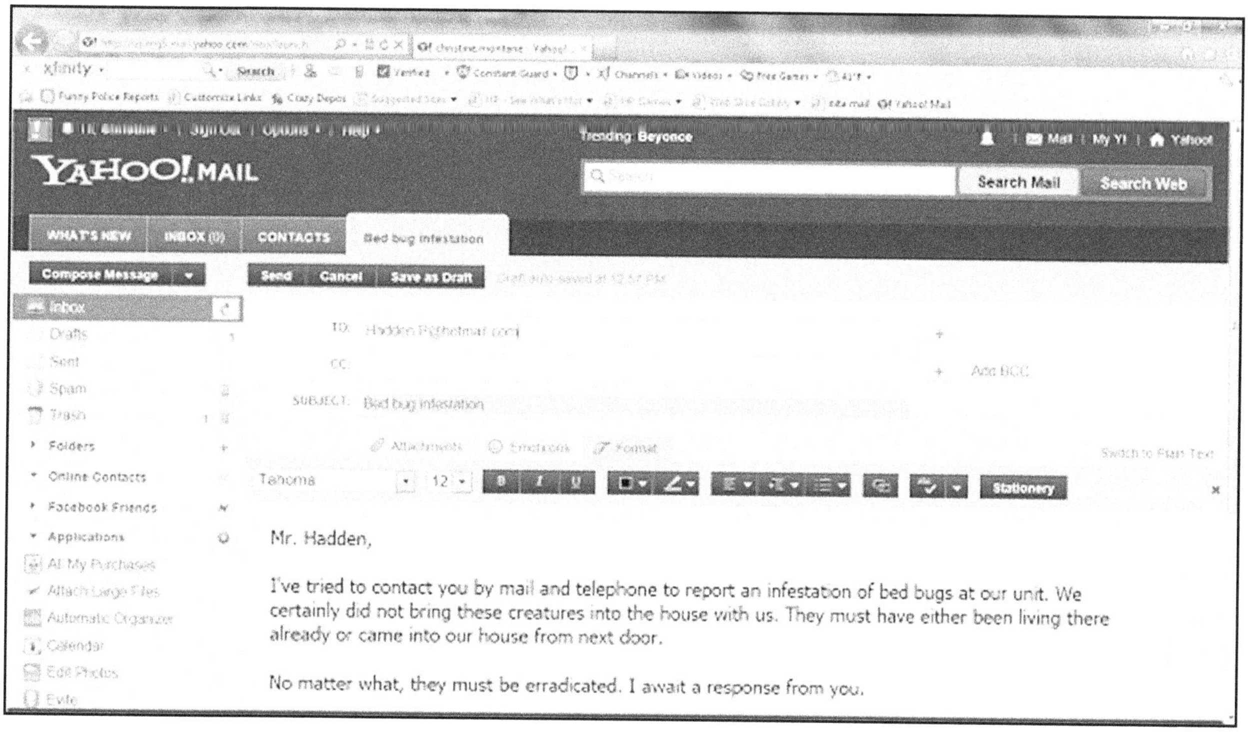

Exhibit 3

PESTCONTROL

34 ANDREWS AVENUE
NITA CITY, NITA
758-5521
WWW.PESTCONTROLOFNITA.COM

24th Day of Month-4

Pat Hadden
Hadden Properties, LLC
4056 17th Court, Suite 250
Nita City, Nita

RE: Job at 890 Front Street, Nita City

Dear Mr. Hadden,

We followed your instructions about contacting the tenant of your property at 890 Front Street to arrange for resolution of a bed bug infestation. I have tried multiple times to contact Ms.Montane and have not been able to reach her. Yesterday, I dropped by the property in an attempt to speak with Ms. Montane in person. In all situations we have been unable to make contact to arrange for a service call.

At this point we are discontinuing our attempts to reach Ms. Montane. If you can reach her, please have her call me directly so we can arrange a service call and provide the appropriate instructions on how to prepare the unit and her personal property.

I am sorry we have not been able to meet your needs in this situation. We appreciate your business. Please do not hesitate to contact us in the future if you have other pest control needs.

Sincerely,

Whitney Cortner

Whitney Cortner
Customer Service Representative

Exhibit 4

HAND-WRITTEN NOTE FROM JOE SANTINI TO PAT HADDEN

"At Your Service"

Pat,

I dropped by your unit at 890 Front Street on 10th day of Month +4 to talk with Ms. Montane about her problem with bed bugs. When she answered the door she told me that she would never again let me into her house. I tried to explain the thing with her sister was a big mistake but she wouldn't listen.

I don't know what you want me to do. It's pretty clear she won't let me in to do any work. I suggest you contact an extermination service. I know the folks at Pest Control and they are good people. They have this new system of heat treatment that is pretty slick – but expensive. Call me if you want their number.

Joe

Exhibit 5

Duplex at 890 Front Street, Nita City, Nita
Taken 18th day of Month-2

Exhibit 6

PHOTOGRAPH OF BED BUG BITES ON JOSEPHINE MONTANE'S ARM
TAKEN ON 5TH DAY OF MONTH-4

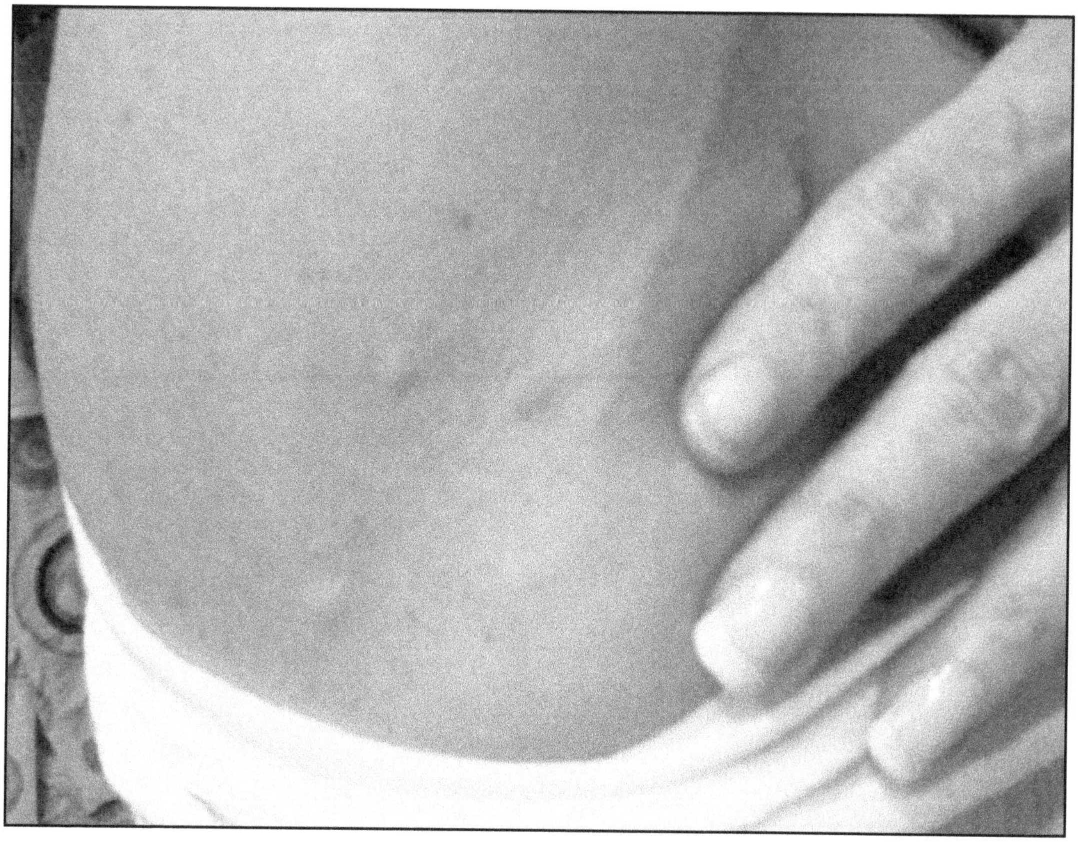

Exhibit 7

PHOTOGRAPH OF BED BUGS INFESTING 890 FRONT STREET TAKEN 5TH DAY OF MONTH-4

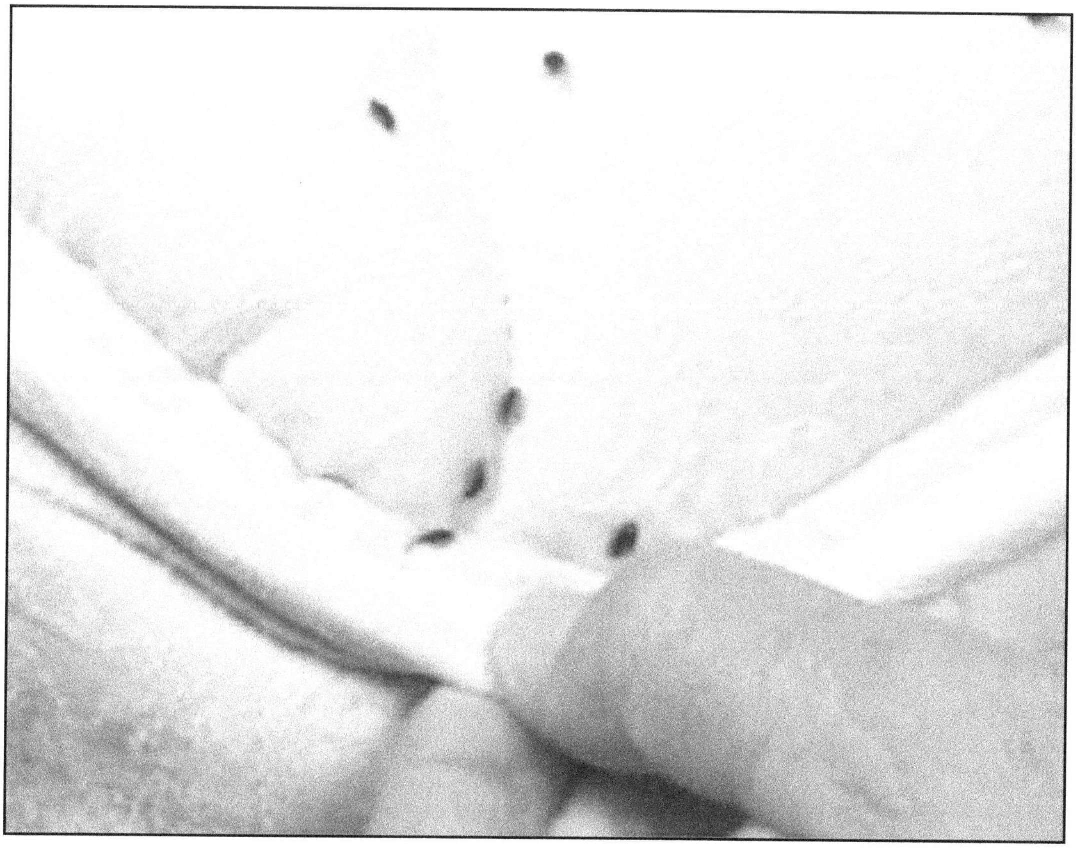

Exhibit 8

PHOTOGRAPH OF BED BUG INFESTATION AT 890 FRONT STREET TAKEN 5TH DAY OF MONTH-4

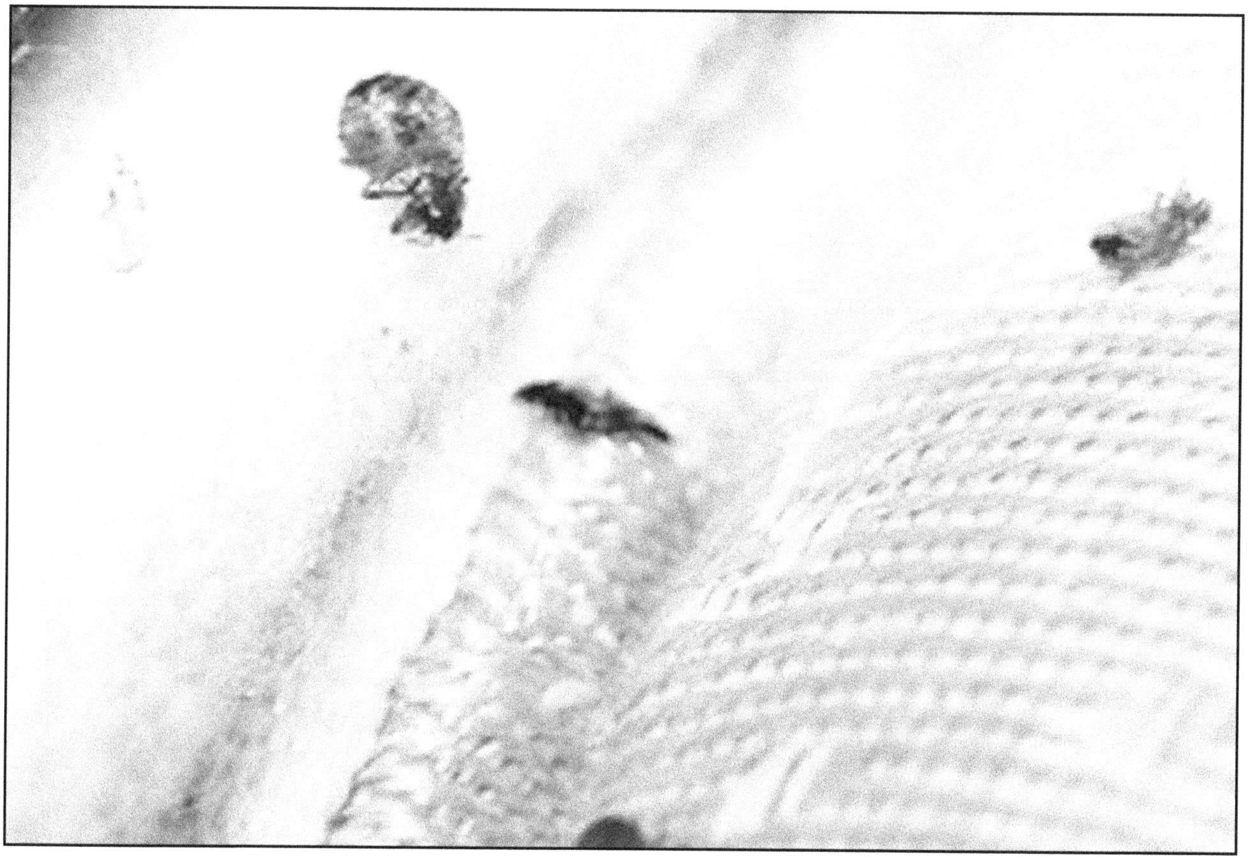

Exhibit 9

Bed bugs discovered at Houston Contract Detention Center
Posted: July 21, YR-1 2:30 PM

By Dave Sisk

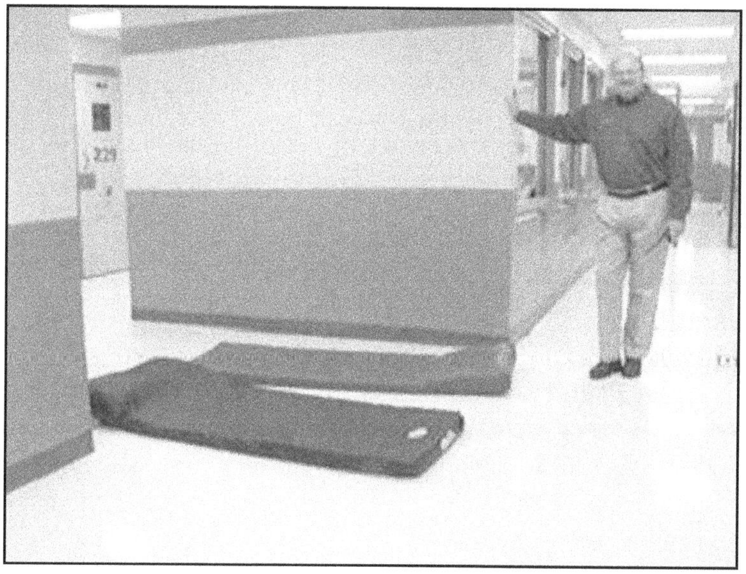

HOUSTON, TX (WIPE) - Bed bugs have invaded the Houston Contract Detention Center.

The bed bug pests just recently showed up at the detention center but officials say they've got it under control.

Health officials say bed bugs have made a national comeback over the past year. Houston Environmental Health Department Director Cletus Oswald explains what they are.

"The short way to put it is they're pests. They're an insect that were pretty common at one time. They were eradicated and now they've made a comeback."

Experts say the age old nighttime creatures do bite, and they like to feed on humans. Bed bugs are normally found in people's bedrooms, or any type of institution where you have a lot of people staying.

The Houston Contract Detention Center has dozens of inmates, and it was an inmate who pointed the bed bugs out to officials.

Jailer Fred Ogborne says they're not sure where the bugs came from, but says he and his staff took action quickly.

"We immediately contacted a professional exterminator. They have treated the infected areas and they're coming back two more times to treat those areas. We removed all the bedding and have either destroyed or sealed it all off. The bed bugs haven't been seen since."

Officials say only three inmates have been affected, but they are not in danger since the bugs don't transmit diseases.

Ogborne tells 5 News they're keeping an eye out for more bugs in the future.

©YR-1 WIPE. All rights reserved. This material may not be published, broadcast, rewritten, or redistributed.

Proposed Jury Instructions

1. The Court will now instruct you on the law governing this case. You must arrive at your verdict by unanimous vote, applying the law as you are now instructed to the facts as you find them to be.

2. The parties in this case are Christine Montane, the plaintiff, and Pat Hadden, the defendant. The parties have agreed, and you must regard as conclusively proven the following facts:

(a) Pat Hadden, is the owner of the property located at 4056 Front Street, Nita City, Nita, the legal description of which is: Lot 4, Baker Subdivision, County of Darrow, Nita City, State of Nita;

(b) Pat Hadden leased the premises to the Christine Montane and her sister on December 1, YR-1, for a term of one year through a written lease.

(c) Rent is due on the first day of each month. Monthly rent is $1,100.00. The rent is current.

3. The Plaintiff, Christine Montane seeks to break her lease with Pat Hadden based upon a claim that Mr. Hadden breached the warranty of habitability for rental properties by failing to keep the building free of vermin or appropriately exterminate such vermin. Her claim is based upon an infestation of bed bugs that she claims were present before she and her sister moved into the property and Hadden's failure to exterminate the vermin.

The Defendant, Pat Hadden, denies he breached any warranty by saying the unit was free of insects before the Montane sisters moved into the property. Hadden claims the Montane sisters, or their frequent guests created the problem by bringing the bed bugs into the unit. He further claims he attempted to remedy the problem on numerous occasions and the Montane sisters refused to grant workers entry. Hadden claims there is no breach and the lease should continue.

4. To find the lease was breached, you must find the following:

(a) The unit located at 4056 Front Street, Nita City, Nita was infested with vermin, specifically bed bugs;

(b) The infestation occurred before the Plaintiff occupied the premises;

(c) The Plaintiff gave adequate notice to the Defendant;

(d) The Defendant had opportunity to correct the problem; and

(e) The Defendant failed to correct the problem.

5. If you find by a preponderance of the evidence that Christine Montane has established her claim, then your verdict should be for the Plaintiff, Christine Montane. Thus if you found the property located at 4056 Front Street, Nita City, Nita was infested by bed bugs on or before December 1, YR-1, and that Pat Hadden failed to correct the problem in a timely fashion, then your verdict should be for the Plaintiff.

6. If you find none of Christine Montane's claims to be supported by a preponderance of the evidence, then your verdict should be for the Defendant, Pat Hadden.

7. The Court did not in any way and does not by these instructions give or intimate any opinions as to what has or has not been proven in the case, or as to what are or not the facts of the case.

You must not be concerned with the wisdom of any rule of law. Regardless of any opinions you may have as to what the law ought to be, it would be a violation of your sworn duty to base a verdict upon any other view of the law than that given in the instructions of the court.

LANDLORD/TENANT COURT, COUNTY OF DARROW, STATE OF NITA

JURY VERDICT FORM

CHRISTINE MONTANE

Plaintiff,

vs.

PAT HADDEN

Defendant.

We, the jury, return the following verdict and each of us concurs in this verdict:

(Choose the appropriate verdict)

a. We, the jury find for the Plaintiff ________________

b. We, the jury find for the Defendant ______________

____

Foreperson

CPSIA information can be obtained
at www.ICGtesting.com
Printed in the USA
FFHW012211170119
50204287-55164FF

9 781601 563231